LIVING IN HARMONY WITH ANIMALS

Practical Tips from

America's #1 Animal Rights Columnist

Carla Bennett

Foreword by
Beatrice Arthur

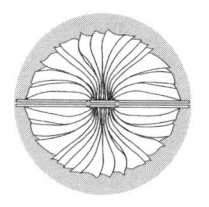

BOOK PUBLISHING COMPANY

SUMMERTOWN, TENNESSEE

© 1999 Carla Bennett

Cover Design: Studio Haus
Interior Design: Warren Jefferson, Michael Cook

Published in the United States by
Book Publishing Company
P.O. Box 99
Summertown, TN 38483
888-260-8458
http://www.bookpubco.com

02 01 00 99   1 2 3 4 5 6

All rights reserved. No portion of this book may be reproduced by any means whatsoever, except for brief quotations in reviews, without permission from the publisher.

ISBN: 1-57067-085-4

Bennett, Carla.
  Living in harmony with animals : practical tips from America's #1 animal rights columnist / Carla Bennett.
    p.   cm.
  ISBN 1-57067-085-4 (alk. paper)
    1. Animal welfare. 2. Human-animal relationships. I. Title.

HV 4735.B46 1999
179'.3--dc21   99-058048

Dedication

"I had felt out-manned, out-gunned, out-financed. But I had used every waking moment to work for what I believed in, and that had been a bigger card than the opposition could offer. I have never felt intimidated by the enormity of the opposition since."

— Ingrid Newkirk, "One Person's Efforts"

This book is dedicated to every activist out there on the "front lines," sometimes all alone in a small town, living a cruelty-free, vegetarian lifestyle and bravely standing up and speaking out for all animals, from a cast-off dog to a starving cat to the billions of beautiful beings out of sight in the meat, vivisection, and fur industry hellholes.

Bravo! You are front runners in the evolution of the human spirit.

Ingrid Newkirk rescued Sheen-Fu from a Taiwan dog pound as he was about to be drowned. Not long after, PETA succeeded in getting Taiwan to pass its first, and far-reaching, animal protection law. Photo by Motoyo Nakamura

Contents

Foreword 8

Preface 10

Chapter 1: Our Wild Neighbors 13

Who's in the Chimney? 14
If You Find a Baby Bird 15
The Scoop on Squirrels 16
A Snake is Someone Too 17
Living Harmoniously with Beavers 18
Wild Animals Can't Be Pets 20
Toads Can't Do the Backstroke 21
Go Wild in Your Yard! 22
Of Mice and Mint 24
Traps of Torture 25
The Town That Lives with Bears 26

Chapter 2: Our Best Buddies 27

How to Choose a Warm, Fuzzy Companion and Make the Relationship Work 28
Bring That "Backyard" Dog Inside 32
Overcoming Allergies with Patience 33
Domesticated Animals Can't Make It on Their Own 34
Are We Listening When Animals Speak? 35
Spay! Neuter! Care! 37
Love Me, Love My Furry Family 38
Truckers' Alert 38
Animals Do Not Live by Bread Alone 39
Dog and Cat Breeders Breed Suffering 41
The Magic of Birds 42
Vaccination Quandaries 44
Training Horses or Torturing Them? 45
When an Animal Is Missing 46
Bunny Huggers 48
Rat Huggers 48

Contents 5

CHAPTER 3: MEALS WITHOUT SQUEALS 50

Rich, Famous, and Tender-Hearted 51
The Rule of Seven 52
Cruelty-Free Is Cholesterol-Free 53
Teen Goes Veg 56
A Pig by Any Other Name Would Be as Sweet 58
Breeding Tigers 59
A Horror d'Oeuvre 60
A Snorkeler's Awakening 62
Save Sea Creatures, Save Yourself 62
What? Tax Meat? 63
Meat: Truth in Labeling 65
Acres and Acres of Animals? 65
Help! There's a Piece of Calf in My Milk! 66
The Joy of Soy 67
Wipe Off That Stupid Milk Mustache 68
Calcium and Bone Loss 69
Holiday Dilemma 70
What That Egg Really Costs 70
That Not-So-Studly Steak 72

CHAPTER 4: SHOPPING: HITTING CORPORATE CRUELTY WHERE IT HURTS 73

Fur is Dead 74
Fur? GRRRRR! 75
Don't Let Anyone Pull the Wool over Your Eyes 77
Walk Away from Leather 78
Down with Feathers 79
Seeing Is Believing 80
Lookin' Good with Conscience 80
Cheap, Cruelty-Free Cleaning 81

CHAPTER 5: TRAVELING? TAKE THE HIGH ROAD 83

Travel Tips from Linda and Kevin Nealon 84
Flying the Unfriendly Skies 85
Animals in Cars: Hotter Than You Think 87
Animal Friendly Getaways 88
Wear Ts, Save the Seas! 89

6 *Living in Harmony with Animals*

CHAPTER 6: THIS IS SPORT? 90

A Psychiatrist Looks at Hunters 91
Hunting Is Hardly Conservation of Wildlife 92
Does Your Favorite Wildlife Charity Support Hunting
   and Trapping? 94
Bonding over Bodies 96
Preserve Us from Hunting Preserves 97
My Dad the Fisherman 98
A Trapper's Opinion of "Dominion" 100

CHAPTER 7: NO FUN FOR THE ANIMALS 101

Backstage at the Big Top 102
Rinky-Dink Roadshow 104
Cruelty for Big Bucks 105
Ridin', Ropin', and Regrettin' 110
Charreadas and One Happy Ending 115
The Bad News about Zoos 113
The Day Willie B. Kissed a Tree 116
The Lure of Aquariums: Don't Bite 117
Bullfights: Tradition of Torture 118
The Greyhound Gig 119
Skip This Ride 120
Rattlesnake Roundups 121
The Shame of Spain 122

CHAPTER 8: IS THIS CUT NECESSARY? 124

Animal Research: Big Business 125
Med School Maneuvers 126
Testing Drugs 127
The Animal Welfare Act 128
Behind Locked Laboratory Doors 128
A Not-So-Noble Nobel Laureate 129
Swallowing Pee (Gulp!) 130

CHAPTER 9: ODDS AND ENDS AND BEGINNINGS 132

A Catholic Nun Speaks Out for the Animals 133
No Souls? No Rights? 134
Convert Your Clergyperson into a Creature Preacher 135
Ending Dissection: One Student's Story 136

Emergency Procedure 137
The Chain of Violence 138
Gruesome Greetings 139
Signs of the Times 139
Life in the (Unbearably) Slow Lane 140
Homebound Activism 140
Yeast and Albert Schweitzer 141
Escaping Blizzardsville 142
Flesh and Blood "Things"? 142
Justice Prevails 144
Seeing's Believing 146
Awareness Shines Forth from All Creatures 147

Appendix 149

Books 149
Magazines 151
Newspaper 152
Catalog 152
Video and Audio Tapes 152
Pro-Animal Groups 154
Additional Web Sites 158
Information on PETA 159

FOREWORD

My introduction to People for the Ethical Treatment of Animals (PETA) came when I agreed to narrate an undercover film their investigators had taken exposing the horrific cruelty of fur farms.

When PETA's director of media Dan Mathews arrived at my home just prior to the taping of my narration, I had just finished viewing the film and was sitting on my living room couch in tears. "I don't know if I can do this," I said, wiping my eyes. He smiled gently and we talked a while about how these animals needed me to speak for them, and about how good I would feel afterward, knowing I had helped them. I went ahead with the narration, and he was right; I felt great afterward, knowing I had helped these poor innocent animals.

I've been helping ever since, whenever and wherever I can. Presently, I am leading PETA's campaign against Premarin, getting the word out to women about how tens of thousands of mares and their foals suffer and die in the production of this cruel product made from pregnant mares' urine, and the wonderful natural alternatives to Premarin now available.

Living in Harmony with Animals is a gold mine of information about all the ways we all can help. Carla Bennett has been with PETA 12 years. As its senior writer and "Kindness Consultant" for PETA's *Animal Times* magazine, she knows the animals, the issues, and the answers. Her "Ask Carla" column in *Animal Times* is the place many readers say they turn to first. This book is a compilation of those columns, plus additional questions, plus more expansive answers than space allows in the magazine.

Here is a book to own as a permanent part of your library, to refer to often, and, because of its broad appeal, to give to others as gifts.

None of us can become Gandhi overnight, but this book tells how each of us can make a huge difference for the animals by our day-to-day shopping, eating, and entertainment choices, and its colorful true stories showcasing animals' intelligence and emotions greatly heighten our awareness of these beautiful creatures' needs. You don't need a lot of time or a lot of money; you just need the knowledge found here.

So please, join all of us who are speaking and acting on behalf of those who can't speak for themselves. You may not want to march into hell, as some have, for this heavenly cause, but I guarantee that no matter how little or how much you give, you will get back more than you give. You will come to know, as I have, what the great humanitarian Dr. Albert Schweitzer felt when he wrote, "I am thrown by reverence for life into an unrest which the world does not know. I receive from it a blessedness which the world cannot give."

Godspeed!

— Beatrice Arthur

A "Golden Girl" with a heart of gold, actress Beatrice Arthur, shown here with her dog Jennifer, is one of PETA's most active spokespersons for animals. Photo by David Goldner

Preface

Since I came to work for PETA 12 years ago, I've been in touch with thousands of "animal" people. They have taught me so much. You'll read about many of them in this book; they deserve the credit for it.

We can help animals in so many ways that take neither time nor money, just knowledge and consideration. Do you know, for example, how your choice of a household or office product or a cosmetic product affects rabbits and other animals in laboratories? Should your circus choice be Ringling Bros. and Barnum & Bailey or the Cirque du Soleil? What if a raccoon builds her nest in your chimney? In what ways does every step you take toward vegetarianism help the animals, your health, and our planet? (I've included some simple, delicious recipes too.) Does the national "animal" organization you belong to support hunting and trapping? (You might be surprised.)

When I remember the special animals in my life, I always think of Butterscotch. This tan and white hen would come running down the path to meet me as fast as her little legs could carry her. At my feet, she would hop up and down, a bouncing featherball, until I picked her up and cuddled her in my arms. There she would nestle cozily, tilt her head, and look up at me with the clear message: "Isn't this nice?"

Bird lovers know that, like Butterscotch, every bird has a unique personality. Dog and cat lovers know each dog and cat does too. So, an aquarium curator has assured me, does every fish.

Imagine! Every animal on Earth has his or her own personality—it boggles my mind! I didn't learn this fact until I'd passed 40, but had I stopped to reason it out earlier, I'd have realized that what was true for every companion animal I ever knew had to be true throughout nature.

To me, this makes humane treatment of animals all the more vital. They aren't "rodeo animals" or "meat animals" or "laboratory animals," they're as individual as you and I, be they calm, high-strung, friendly, independent, shy, brave, or their own special mix of these and other characteristics.

Take Jet Frost, for example. The stress of horse racing was too much for this beautiful two-year-old thoroughbred, and she had a nervous breakdown. She refused to run or do anything except stand in her stall facing the wall. In short order, her corporate owners scheduled this sensitive youngster to be sold to the charreadas—rodeos that cruelly trip horses and break their legs before sending them on to slaughter. But at the last minute, Jet Frost got lucky. You'll find her story in Chapter 7.

The industries that use and exploit animals today are careful to keep their dirty secrets under wraps and to present a humane image to the public. Many of us have helped them by not wanting to know what goes on behind the scenes. Their public relations people are the best big money can buy, but even they can't hold up under the spotlight of truth. In this book, I've told the truth about these industries but have not dwelled on it. I'd rather accentuate the positive: share the ways we can help animals and, in doing so, set examples for others, make some collective waves for the future, and, along the journey, experience the wonderful feeling that comes with compassionate living.

Thank you for caring

— Carla Bennett

Acknowledgements

Thanks to Ingrid Newkirk for giving me the work that fulfilled my heart's desire, for being an unstoppable inspiration, for encouraging me to write this book, and for fine-tuning many of the items in it.

Thanks to Peter Singer for writing *Animal Liberation* and Alex Pacheco and Ingrid Newkirk for bringing it to life with PETA.

Thanks to Jeanne Roush for her insight, ideas, and steadfast encouragement.

Thanks to everyone in my PETA Headquarters "family" especially Alisa Mullins, Karin Bennett, Kathy Guillermo, Alison Green, Paula Moore, Anna West, Karen Porreca, Robyn Wesley, Jenny Woods, Peter Wood, Tal Ronnen, Kristina Johnson, and Joey Penello for their ideas and help.

Thanks to my kids Kristin Bennett, Karin Bennett, and Mark Helsen for their love, support, and great senses of humor.

Thanks to Ann Pacheco for being my sounding board and believing in this book.

Thanks to Claudine Erlandson and Nancy Pennington for their support and unstoppable activism for animals.

Thanks to Jon Wynne-Tyson for *The Extended Circle, A Dictionary of Humane Thought*; my treasured autographed copy is worn ragged.

Thanks to Bob Holzapfel for publishing this book with no holds barred, Cynthia Holzapfel, Michael Cook, and Warren Jefferson for producing it with heart as well as expertise, and Anna Casini for her supportive promotional work. I am grateful to have had the opportunity to work with them. Their own wonderful work for animals includes making animal-friendly books and vegetarian food products and books available far and wide, including via mail order.

Thanks to Carol Lorente for her superb editing.

Chapter 1

🐾 🐾 🐾

Our Wild Neighbors

Who's In The Chimney?

> *People create far more problems for wild animals than the animals create for people, and most problems are the results of humans' interference in a natural system.*
>
> —Sally Joosten, Wildlife Rehabilitator

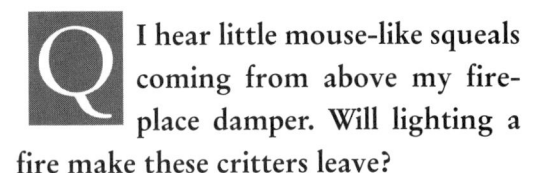

Q I hear little mouse-like squeals coming from above my fireplace damper. Will lighting a fire make these critters leave?

— Mark M.

A No! You'll burn them alive! I'll bet a veggie burger you're hearing baby raccoons. Few animals can climb up and down slippery chimney flues, but clever Mom Raccoon puts her seat against one side and her feet against the opposite side and inches her way up and down.

This little family is in your chimney because we humans have cut down so many old granddaddy trees that raccoons use for their homes or dens.

If for some reason you can't wait for them to leave, you can put a radio turned to loud talk or rock music in the fireplace and hang a mechanic's trouble light down your chimney. Give Mom a week or so to find a new home and move her babies. Then have your chimney professionally capped, first making sure they're all out. Hell hath no fury like a mother raccoon separated from her baby—she'll tear your roof apart.

This radio-light-patience technique also works with animals in your attic or under your porch. They like their dens dark and quiet. It also saves the animals from being separated, even temporarily, like the ones John Hammond trapped. John, a compassionate, licensed wildlife relocator and chimney sweep, was called upon to remove a raccoon family from a garage loft. First, he caught three little raccoons. He trapped their mom later in a live trap. To reunite her with her babies, he placed the trap against their cage. As he went to open the doors of both, Mom saw her kids. She chirruped with joy and bounced up and down. Who says animals have no feelings?

Personally, I'd prop a sturdy stick or other brace under the damper to keep it securely in place, relax, and let this family be. When the youngsters are about eight weeks old, they and Mom will move out to enjoy their small portion of Earth, sun, and life. That is the time to have the chimney capped.

IF YOU FIND A BABY BIRD

Q I saw a plump baby robin teetering on a fence around a cement parking lot and became worried about his immediate future. But there were no bushes or trees nearby to move him to, so I left him alone. Was this wrong?

— Neil O.

> *"Man is not the lord of all the world's animals. He is the protector."*
>
> — John Forsythe

A As the man said when the phone booth collapsed, it's a hard call. Sometimes you can move a fledgling in obvious danger to a nearby branch; other times you just have to trust Mom and Dad Bird to pull everything off.

Keep dogs and cats away from fledglings. These little birds can't fly well, so they sit still on the ground a lot, trying not to be seen. During this critical time with their parents, they learn lifetime survival skills.

A half-inch or more of tail feathers indicates that a youngster has flown the coop, or fledged. You needn't bother putting him back in the nest, because once he's fledged, fledge he will again, just like toast popping from the toaster.

But if he has no feathers or just a little fuzz, pick him up very gently and put him back in his nest. Don't worry, your scent on him won't keep his parents away.

If the nest is unreachable, you can make him one out of a berry basket, kitchen strainer, or small plastic container with holes punched in the bottom. Line it with shredded tissue—not cotton, grass, hay, or straw, because they can cause respiratory problems. Don't use old bird nests, either; they may contain parasites. Hang it in a sheltered place near the original nest, no farther than five feet, if possible. Get out of sight and watch to make sure the parents return.

For more detailed information about rescuing baby birds, send for PETA's free pamphlet, "Emergency Care for Baby Birds."

THE SCOOP ON SQUIRRELS

> *"If an animal does something, we call it instinct; if we do the same thing for the same reason, we call it intelligence."*
>
> —Will Cuppy

Q I heard the patter of tiny feet on the other side of my ceiling, and then several days later, I was standing in my yard looking at my house when suddenly I saw a little squirrel face poking out from a small hole in my attic vent. I'm wondering if there are squirrels with babies up there. What should I do?

— J. J.

A Baby squirrels are born as early as March and stay in the nest 10 to 12 weeks. Normally there are three babies. Parents may have a second litter in the fall. So about the first week of June, after the family has exited for the day, plug up that hole and any others you might see. Make sure everyone is out, though. Mom Squirrel will wreak havoc on your roof to save one of her children.

Then, if you have no squirrel-stalking dogs or cats lurking around the neighborhood, you can give the squirrels some fun and yourself some entertainment. Tie a length of thick, frayed rope to a low branch, so the squirrels can jump up and catch the frayed end from the ground. They'll love using this as a swing.

~ ~ ~

A Snake Is Someone Too

Q My brother feeds his snake live mice! He puts them in the terrarium with the snake, and the poor dear mice press against the back glass—sometimes for days—frozen in terror, until the snake gets hungry and eats them. I told my brother this is barbaric, but he insists snakes need live food.

> "... and a mouse is miracle enough to stagger sextillions of infidels."
> —Walt Whitman

— S.R.

A "Wrong," says Dale Marcellini, curator of reptiles at the National Zoo in Washington, D.C. "Snakes get accustomed to eating dead prey." He went on to tell me that all 300 snakes at the National Zoo are fed dead prey, often taken from the freezer and thawed. Other snakes will eat canned dog food.

"For the rare individual snake that wants movement," said Marcellini, "we use forceps to hold out the dead prey and wiggle it."

Of course, in nature, the ordeal you describe rarely happens to mice. They either get away or never know what hit them.

This is one more example of why exotic animals should not be in captivity. Also, it is extremely unfair to the snake to make him spend his one and only life in a prison. Urge your brother to check with a herpetologist for a suitable area into which to release the snake during spring or summer.

Incidentally, I always feared snakes until several years ago. Near a crumbling, low brick wall attached to an unused outdoor barbecue pit 20 feet or so from our back door, I saw a slender little garter snake about seven inches long. She was basking in the sun, but staying close enough to a nearby small hole in the brick wall to slip into it in case of danger. Containing my impulse to scream and run, I made a mental note not to mow close to the wall in that place.

Sure enough, I saw her there throughout the summer, sunning herself, never going far from her home, and certainly never causing me or any of my housemates the least trouble. I also learned that almost all snakes are shy creatures who will do everything in their power to avoid you and will bite only as a last resort. They are also very helpful in controlling insect populations.

Living Harmoniously With Beavers

"All great discoveries are made by people whose feelings run ahead of their thinking."
— C. H. Parkhurst

Q Some members of our subdivision property owners association want to hire a trapper to kill the beavers who have built a dam in our lake and damaged some ornamental trees. Can you provide a better solution?

— Sick at Heart

A Don't blame beavers for doing what comes naturally. Often they will be attracted to a subdivision lake, especially if the property owners have planted some tasty ornamental trees around it. The solution: Wrap protection around what's left of these trees, and don't plant any more. After all, it's the beavers' land too.

If the beavers have built a dam that's causing shore land to flood, here's a solution. Scores of individuals, municipalities, and oil and gas companies have used beaver bafflers with resounding success and have saved thousands of dollars in the process. These simple wire cylinders keep beavers from plugging up culverts, causing road washouts, or flooded land or well sites. They also control the size of beavers' dams.

Beavers are extremely gentle. Beaver expert and lecturer Sherri Tippie reports being able to handle many she has live-trapped. She doesn't recommend this, though. You could get a frightened beaver who could hurt you. Several she held in her apartment overnight padded from her bathtub to her living room and curled up next to her cat.

Beaver expert Sherri Tippie holding young wild beaver she has just live trapped for relocation.

Beavers mate for life, and their youngsters stay with them for two years and then maintain a lifelong relationship with them. Beavers are also extremely beneficial to the environment, and many landowners want them on their property.

Jeanne Roush also learned first-hand how gentle beavers are. As PETA's Director of Research and Investigations, Jeanne flew to Stevensville, Mont., to investigate a complaint about the Crum beaver "ranch," a 20-acre tract littered with tiny cement cells in which beavers were bred, then bludgeoned for their skins. Caretakers had walked off the job, and the absentee owners had made no provisions to feed the animals. Jeanne arrived to find that 1,100 animals had already starved to death and the remaining beavers were in various stages of starvation.

"The smell of death was everywhere," said Jeanne. "Worse were their faces. I'll never forget them. The beavers looked right at us, making eye contact, and I could see their pain. After all they had endured, they were friendly and gentle to us. We spoke softly to give reassurance. They seemed to understand and accept us completely."

A free packet of information about co-existing with beavers, including information on beaver sterilization programs and how to protect trees, is available from PETA.

WILD ANIMALS CAN'T BE PETS

> *"Love a wild animal enough to do what is best for him."*
> — Sally Joosten, Wildlife Rehabilitator

Q Would it be okay to catch a baby fox and raise him to be my pet? I would take wonderful care of him.

— Danny O.

A Appealing as a wild animal youngster may be, don't try to tame him. It's unfair, because:

* He needs to be and learn with others of his own kind.
* At maturity, when he grows wilder, you most likely will want to give him his freedom. By this time, he'll have lost one of his greatest protections—the fear of people. Then the first person he trustingly approaches will most likely think, "Rabies!" A wild creature suspected of being rabid isn't given 10 days of "rabies observation," as dogs and cats are. He's killed immediately, and his head is sawed off and sent to a laboratory for examination.
* Keeping a wild animal is against the law in most places.

Sometimes you may see a young animal whose mom has been killed. If so, call a licensed wildlife rehabilitator. (You did put the phone number of one in your wallet, didn't you?)

Most wild animals stay hidden, even on warm summer days. But if their dens get hot, they may come outside. Foxes have been known to stretch out on patios. You may also see opossums, woodchucks, skunks, rabbits, chipmunks, and an occasional raccoon during the daytime, especially in summer. One steamy afternoon, I spotted a raccoon sprawled on a branch high overhead, gazing down at me.

A normally nocturnal adult animal seen during the day should be observed from a safe distance. If he hurries away from you, chances are he's healthy. If he's lethargic, walks slowly, or staggers, he may be sick. Distemper is more often the culprit than rabies. Unlike rabies, distemper is not contagious to humans. In its early stages, it makes for mucousy nose and eyes; later an animal may get seizures, and then distemper becomes more difficult to tell from rabies.

However, an animal never has what one man called "distemper tantrums!"

Toads Can't Do The Backstroke

Q Every so often, I find a dead mouse, toad, or frog in our swimming pool. It makes me very sad to think how they must have struggled and swum endlessly to find a way out. What can I do?

— Jason T.

> *"I'm sure I've been a toad, one time or another. With bats, weasels, worms. I rejoice in the kinship. Even the caterpillar I can love, and the various vermin."*
>
> — Theodore Roethke "Slug"

A Call (800) 483-4366 and order one or several of PETA's toadally awesome Frog Saver Lilypads. Animals trapped in pools swim around the edge, searching for avenues of escape. Snapped onto your pool ladder or attached to the wall, this attractive "lilypad" gives them the leg up they need. Also, to give other trapped beings a way out, prop sturdy sticks in open window wells, twigs in birdbaths or water buckets, and branches in dumpsters. Animals such as raccoons and cats often get in dumpsters and then, because dumpsters have slippery sides, they can't climb out.

In 1995, a column of migrating toads more than 1,000 miles long wound its way through China; residents of Benxl watched in amazement as the toads traveled along the Taize River.

Most of the toads were newly born and no longer than a fingernail. The larger ones were spaced out every 30 feet, leading the others along. Said one witness, "The toads seemed disciplined. Once one tried to stop, the others would push him on."

I had a toad friend once. When I would sit on my patio step in Illinois in the late evenings of summer, a large toad who lived among our rose bushes would invariably emerge and sit beside me. Sometimes I petted him or picked him up momentarily. I have no doubt that he was being companionable. A person I told this to joked that I should have kissed the toad and maybe he would have turned into a psychiatrist! But I swear my story is true. I really did have a toad friend.

GO WILD IN YOUR YARD!

> "As cruel a weapon as the cave man's club, the chemical barrage has been hurled against the fabric of life."
> — Rachel Carson, author and environmentalist

Q How can I make my yard more animal-friendly?
— J. L.

A To put life in your yard, save dead wood. Snags (dead trees) and stumps are crucial to kicking our pesticide habit and solving the increasing dilemma of pesticide resistance. For birds and small mammals (Mother Nature's phenomenal insect controllers), dead trees, stumps, and logs are ecological gold. More than 150 species of creatures nest in them and feed on their insect tenants and other insects in your yard. These birds and animals include nuthatches, woodpeckers, squirrels, raccoons, bluebirds, owls, chickadees, wood ducks, and wrens.

Top off, don't chop down, snags 12 inches or more in diameter and away from the house. The thicker the tree, the better. Be sure to check for nests and dens first! Check for occupants, too, before you call a tree-trimming company. Spring is nesting time and these are the animals' homes. If you find any, leave the snag alone for a few weeks until the babies are grown and on their own. A mother raccoon in Maryland was chain-sawed in half because she stayed with her babies in a tree being cut down.

As elegant, snag-nesting swallows, swifts, and purple martins sweep through the air, mosquitoes will disappear from your yard. Huge great-granddaddy den trees are also homes for peregrine falcons, barn owls, and ivory-billed woodpeckers.

Increasingly, corporations and apartment complex owners are planting lawns only in the areas immediately around their buildings. They're leaving the outer areas of their property woodsy and natural, with tall grasses, wildflowers, evergreens, hedgerows, and bushes to provide cover and homes to wildlife. Homeowners can do this on a smaller scale in their yards.

Speaking of lawns, all this will be for naught unless you avoid putting chemicals on your yard. Lawn chemicals poison the Earth and all its creatures. They poison the yard they're applied to and also travel via storm drains, streams, and toxic clouds to poison other areas.

A chemical-free lawn, like a tree, detoxifies the air of pollutants and brings better health to four- and two-legged property occupants. A lot of unseen underground activity by worms and microorganisms makes a lawn healthy. If you allow this biological activity to go on unharmed by pesticides, roots will be stronger and chemical fertilizers unnecessary.

Lawns can survive with little or no fertilizer. There are now excellent organic fertilizers on the market, but beware of harmful petroleum-based products that are represented as "organic" because they contain a little manure.

24 *Living in Harmony with Animals*

Remember, in a natural, healthy lawn, the grass will be slower-growing, stronger, and more drought-resistant.

And don't worry about dandelions or other weeds. Weeds are judgment calls. Dig them out by hand if you don't like them, and be grateful for the exercise and chance to spend time in your healthy yard.

Plant a mix of shrubs, trees, and flowers that will provide nuts, berries, seeds, and nectar to birds and other wildlife throughout the year. Holly bushes, for instance, provide winter berries for food, winter foliage for cover, and places to raise young.

Rocks and leaf and brush piles away from the house also provide cover and places to raise young. A small pond with shallow ends for the birds, away from trees and bushes, makes a good water supply. Edge it with water plants. Locate it where you can watch the wildlife activity from a window all year long.

Even a window-box planter can be beneficial and entertaining. One containing marigolds, zinnias, or red salvia can attract butterflies and hummingbirds. A butterfly bush (Buddleiaja davidji) is irresistible to butterflies, those enchanting beauties who become rarer each year.

Happy co-existing!

OF MICE AND MINT

> *"Until we stop harming all other living beings, we are still savages."*
> — Thomas A. Edison

Q Mice abandoned my kitchen cupboards after I put cotton balls soaked in oil of peppermint in them.

— Pat G.

A A tip of the hat to you, Pat, for this great tip. It's always best to find ways to make wild animals move themselves, rather than trap them and move them. And once they're gone, make sure all food is in sealed, rodent-proof, glass, metal, or ceramic containers, and seal up any and all holes through which they might be entering.

Should the oil of peppermint fail to work, buy a humane live trap to relocate the mice. PETA sells such a trap under the name "Smart Mouse Trap."

TRAPS OF TORTURE

Q Yesterday, I opened one of my grandfather's kitchen drawers and my heart broke. There was a mouse struggling in a sticky glue trap. She actually had had babies in the glue. The babies were lifeless, and the mother mouse's delicate little legs were mired in the glue. I watched, horrified, as she rubbed an eye with one glue-covered paw and got glue in her eye and then all over her tiny face. She was squeaking so pitifully!

My brother was there and he killed her. Then I made my grandfather swear he would never put out a glue trap again.

Please tell people to never, ever, use glue traps.

— Sad

> *"Animals depend on us to be their guardian angels."*
> — Actress Sara Gilbert

A If I had my way, people selling or using glue traps would go to jail for extreme cruelty to animals. Mice, squirrels, rats, kittens, and birds all get caught in these horrors. Please, friends, when you see glue traps in a store, complain to the manager and say you won't be back until they are removed. Encourage him or her to instead stock humane live traps, with air holes, so the animals can be released unharmed.

Even better, tell him about Pat G.'s tip (page 24-25) and ask him to stock oil of peppermint and cotton balls in the trap section! Sometimes, all you need do to make a miracle happen is ask for it.

THE TOWN THAT LIVES WITH BEARS

> *"This is a town that wants to get along with nature."*
> — Michael Donnelly, Chief of Police, Mammoth Lakes, Calif.

Q Can people co-exist with large wild animals?
— Cindy R.

A Mammoth Lakes, Calif., has 30 to 40 black bears inside its six-square-mile boundaries. They're in the foundation of the Travelodge motel, in the halfway house breezeway, and under a score of other buildings.

In "Town Bears," a fascinating article in the Dec. 14, 1997, *Seattle Post-Intelligencer*, Frank Clifford described how the bears wander the streets, oblivious to traffic. The town prohibits hunting within the town limits and also inside a large perimeter surrounding the town.

"This is a town that wants to get along with nature. It may be naive when it comes to bears, but that's what we have set out to do: live with them—at a safe distance, " said Police Chief Michael Donnelly. Neither he nor any of his officers hunt.

The town hired trapper Steve Searles to control the bears, which he does with pepper spray, rubber bullets, and exploding flares. He knows all the bears and has given them names. They recognize him and his truck, and some run when they see it coming.

Donnelly and Searles are working to get people to use bear-proof garbage containers and stop putting out food for them, but not everyone cooperates. Donnelly said one woman refers to the bears as "my dogs" and puts out dog food for them. "We're trying to change attitudes like that," he said.

CHAPTER 2

Our Best Buddies

Longtime PETA supporter Candice Bergen hugs Oliver, one of the dogs rescued from a Missouri dog dealer by PETA investigator Kyle Owen.

How To Choose A Warn, Fuzzy Companion And Make The Relationship Work

> "A kitten is more amusing than half the people one is obliged to live with."
>
> —Lady Sydney Morgan

Do you hanker to hear the patter of little feet? Four of them?

If you're planning to bring a hairy being into your life, remember: The key word is "being," as opposed to "thing." Big or little, fuzzy or smooth, this animal guy or gal is going to have his or her own individual personality and unique way of looking at the world and relating to you. Since you're taking his life into your hands, he's going to need your commitment to a long-term relationship, some of your time every day, and a chunk of your paycheck. Everyone who's going to live with the animal should want him; too many times, people get an animal just to "teach the kids responsibility," and the animal ends up ignored and often unfed. But with forethought and care, you can make this a win-win relationship that will add a priceless amount of joy to both your lives for years to come.

Need I say we're talking inside companion? Outside is out. Banishing a dog to a life outside, away from his people (his pack) is too, too mean. And a cat who runs amok outdoors too often gets squished under a car, poisoned, kidnapped for resale to a laboratory, lost, shot, or tortured to death.

Whether you start with just one animal or take the plunge and bring home two, plan to shell out a sizable amount to a veterinarian for physical exams and shots. Also, have an animal spayed or neutered at the earliest possible age, so that he or she will be less frustrated and less frustrating to you, less prone to disease, and will not be producing unwanted offspring to add to the tremendous pet overpopulation problem. Some animal shelters have low-cost spay-neuter programs, as do many humane societies and that wonderful organization, SPAY/USA. (Call (800) 248-SPAY.)

There are many fine animal shelters with a variety of animals, one more appealing than the next, occasionally including hamsters, guinea pigs, rabbits, and birds. But here, we'll focus on dogs and cats.

Whether you want an adorable mutt, an alley cat (who will automatically be beautiful or handsome, because that's the only way cats are made), or a particular breed, check the shelters. Approximately one-third of the dogs and a smaller percentage of the cats there are purebreds. Other sources for purebreds are breed rescue clubs; ask the shelter manager or your local humane society where to contact one. Don't patronize a pet shop or private breeder, because, sure as pouring gasoline on a blazing fire, you will be helping them add to our tragic pet overpopulation. Furthermore, pet shops have a horrible record of selling overpriced, inbred, often sick puppies obtained from the deplorable puppy mills.

Personally, my first choice is a mixed breed. As writer Mike Capuzzo put it so well, mutts are the Hondas of the dog world. This goes for cats and the cat world too.

A point in favor of a mutt is that he or she is not predisposed to certain problems that purebreds are. Many specific breeds have been overbred and inbred to the point where physical or disposition problems have emerged.

When considering dog breeds, keep in mind that a big dog needs more walking than a little dog. A little one gets much of his exercise just walking around the house. If you plan to jog with your dog, remember that he needs to build up his stamina gradually and can become overheated fast. If the two of you exercise in the morning, he will be more content to lie around the house all day while you're at work (unless you work at a nice place like PETA headquarters, where well-behaved companion animals are welcome).

Many people who work full-time opt for a cat, or cats, since cats use litter boxes and don't have to be walked, although they might enjoy donning a harness and leading you around outside by the end of a long leash to satisfy their curiosity about the outside world. Never tie a cat up outside—he could be attacked by a dog or hang himself. Also remember that cats can and do fall from balconies and are badly injured or killed.

Speaking of litter boxes, almost all kittens and cats will "automatically" use them, provided the litter is scooped daily and changed often. A cat who suddenly begins avoiding a clean litter box and "squatting" in various parts of the home may have a bladder infection and should be seen by a veterinarian immediately. Delay can be fatal, especially for a male cat.

Declawed cats are also more likely to relieve themselves in places other than a litter box, so for that reason, and others, don't declaw a cat. Declawing takes away one of a cat's best defenses. Also, the cat will quickly learn to bite, for obvious reasons, and his "stubs" will be sensitive. A couple of scratching posts or corrugated cardboard boxes should keep your furniture intact.

Should you get a cat or a kitten? If you get a kitten, I guarantee he will sleep all day and be wide awake all night. And so will you, because he'll be pouncing on your toes, teasing you to play with him.

The solution? Get an adult cat, or better yet, two. These fascinating creatures aren't as demanding as a kitten or a dog, but they are social (think prides of lions) and like companionship.

The same goes for any animals who have to be alone all day. Two's company, whether they're cats, dogs, or one of each. (Most dogs and cats can become fast friends.) Introduce all animals to each other cautiously, and supervise their getting-acquainted period.

Disciplining Your Companion

Like children, dogs need to be taught right from wrong, so sign up for obedience classes. Your local shelter or park department can tell you when and where they are held.

Never hit an animal. For any reason. Not even with a rolled-up newspaper. It makes him fearful and confused. Being hit is the main reason dogs bite and one of the main reasons cats bite and scratch. If you have children, let them know in no uncertain terms that they must never abuse or overhandle the animal.

Well-known animal therapist and psychic Lydia Hiby says animals understand positive communication far better than negative. Rather than say to a dog, "Don't bark," say: "Be quiet." Don't say: "Get off the couch;" say: "Stay on the floor."

An animal responds to your excitement, says Hiby, so don't get excited when he does something bad. Rather, "get crazy" and praise him with exuberance when he behaves well. He will soon begin to figure out how he can get more of this fun attention.

She also says—and I believe her—that animals think in pictures just as people do, and when they are watching us, they are reading our minds. Try "imaging" things to them. You can also try to "read" psychically what animals, even fish, are thinking or feeling. Hiby says we are all capable of this, that it just takes practice. Trust your first impression—it's usually right. She also says that verbalizing what you want—remembering to be positive—reinforces your desire to the animal.

Keep in mind that most animals communicate subtly. Dogs say so much with their eyes. Cats' little mews are questions or acknowledgments of their enjoyment of your attention or some other personal communication with you. It took me an embarrassingly long time to figure out that when Rudy, our black cat, laid his ears back, he wasn't feeling mean; he was just listening to see if we were following him.

There is so much more to know about living with animals that I urge you to get some books about it. Two excellent ones are The Urban Dog, *by Patricia Curtis, and* 250 Ways to Make Your Cat Adore You, *by Ingrid Newkirk.*

Here's wishing you and your animal companions good times, good health, and many, many good years together.

Bring That "Backyard" Dog Inside

> "Millions of canines in these United States live their entire lives—24 hours a day, seven days a week, 365 days a year—in chains. The land of the free is still home of the chain for many of man's best friends."
>
> — Alisa Mullins

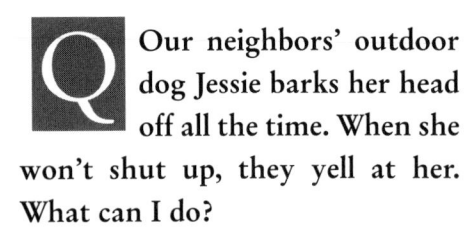

Q Our neighbors' outdoor dog Jessie barks her head off all the time. When she won't shut up, they yell at her. What can I do?

— Al J.

A Jessie is starved for affection. Thousands of years ago people lived together in small groups, and dogs did too. People and animals are both pack animals.

Today's dogs have no canine packs to live with, so they need to be with their human families. A barking, whining "outside" dog like Jessie is desperately trying to get her family's attention. In time, the stress of solitary confinement may make her fearful or vicious or in some other way terribly disturbed, like a big old rust-colored mixed Chow a friend told me about.

This poor dog was chained in the backyard of a Cambridge, Md., home for 13 years, ever since he was a puppy. Into the ground he had worn a circle that outlined the circumference of his chain, a wide, dusty, bare-ground circle that marked his endless straining to get off that chain. Kids who went through the alley teased him by poking sticks at him. During his thirteenth year, the rusty, old chain finally broke. And do you know what? That poor old dog who had wanted his freedom all his life started running—around and around the circle he had worn into the ground. He ran and ran around that circle until he dropped dead of a heart attack.

Jessie needs to be brought into the home, patiently house trained, and taken to obedience classes, if necessary. She needs to have someone accept her gifts of devotion, friendship, and love and take the time to return them.

Show your neighbors this chapter. Perhaps Jessie just doesn't fit into their lifestyle. Maybe she was an unwanted gift. Whatever, the case, if they can't give her the attention she needs, perhaps they will let you either take her into your home or find her a new home with someone else. If there is no other home for her, she should be taken to a reputable animal shelter.

A sad, lonely dog always kept outside is suffering, and who wants to maintain such suffering?

(You may want to copy this and send or give it to others who keep dogs chained or isolated outside.)

OVERCOMING ALLERGIES WITH PATIENCE

Q I have allergies. Does this mean I can never have a companion animal?

— J. L.

A Allergies are nothing to sneeze at. But too often people, including doctors, assume an animal is causing an allergic reaction without investigating further. And sometimes they are mistaken. But even if they're not, there's hope.

> *"Real Cats would rather die than show enthusiasm, no matter how exciting the occasion. Real Dogs kill themselves with enthusiasm, no matter how dull the event. The only time cats break up with laughter is when they pass a dog obedience school."*
>
> — Don Addis

Sometimes an allergic person can build up a resistance to an individual animal. A friend of mine discovered the charisma of cats when she was in her forties, but each time she added a cat to the household, she and her daughter began sneezing themselves silly. However, they found that by toughing out three weeks of sneezing, wheezing, and watery eyes, they built up a resistance to the new animal and were no longer adversely affected by him. They ended up with four cats, two dogs, and nary a sniffle.

Here are other things to try:

* Desensitize your home. Brush your cat or dog every day, or have someone else brush her. (Cats don't need to be bathed, thank goodness.)
* Let someone else vacuum. If you must vacuum, wear a mask and open a screened window so dust can escape. Increase suction by lightly spraying the carpet with water.
* Use a covered litter box (if your cat will tolerate the cover) and plain, unscented, non-clumping litter.
* Use an air conditioner in summer and a humidifier or ventilation fan in winter.
* Get a good air purifier. One person who had been hospitalized for allergies now lives comfortably and breathes easily even though there are two cats in his home. The air purifier worked for him. Don't buy a small department store model; invest in an "industrial" or more specialized type. Choose a mechanical rather than electrostatic purifier. The latter may produce ozone, an irritant. Check your yellow pages under "Air Cleaning and Purifying Equipment."
* See an allergist for a thorough testing, not just a scratch test. Your insurance may cover this. Animal dander (natural skin dandruff) is just one possible irritant. Other culprits may be dust, pollen, grasses, plant molds, ozone, some foods, perfumes, smoke, and feathers. Because allergens' effects are cumulative, controlling these other irritants may relieve your possible allergic reactions to an animal.
* Feed your animals a high-quality diet so their skin won't flake.
* Eliminate allergy-producing animal products from your own diet.

Try these suggestions one at a time or all at once. You may need only one or two of them.

Good luck!

· · ·

Domesticated Animals Can't Make It On Their Own

Q Please ask people not to buy baby ducks or chicks for Easter or abandon domesticated ducks or geese on ponds, for here they will die a slow death. They can't fly or fend for themselves. They can't live on stale bread, and many are tormented and injured by unruly children.

> *"As the humanlike qualities of birds and other animals penetrate deep into the consciousness of a new generation, humanity's philosophy of life will turn around..."*
>
> — Theodore X. Barber, Ph.D, *The Human Nature of Birds*

I found Mr. Drake huddled on the bank of a frozen pond, left behind by his wild companions. I caught him, stuffed him into a box, and put it into the back of my car. He immediately quacked and flapped his way to the front seat, where the heater was blasting. There he stood with half-closed eyes, uttering low, grateful quacks. He did a dropping, and it was solid—he actually was freezing inside!

That evening, he followed me about, and when I sat down on the floor, he waddled over to me and rested his head on my knee, lifting it now and then to stare at the TV screen.

He lived 13 years. Meantime, I became a licensed wildlife rehabilitator and have rescued many more domesticated and wild waterfowl. Each has his or her own wonderful, distinct personality.

— Donna P.

A Thanks for making your points so eloquently, Donna. Folks, please get the phone numbers of your local wildlife rehabilitators from your humane society and keep them handy in case of emergency.

ARE WE LISTENING WHEN ANIMALS SPEAK?

> "Animals can communicate quite well. And they do. And generally speaking, they are ignored."
> — Alice Walker

Q Do you believe animals try to talk to us?
— D. D.

A There's no doubt of it. Here's a true story from Mrs. K. D. of Big Timber, Mont.:

"Tex, my brother-in-law, has 33 geese and a gander. One day, the geese charged into his farm shop, honking excitedly. Then they ran back and forth to the open door, honking continually. Since they'd never come to the shop before, and since the gander wasn't with them, Tex finally got up and followed them outside. They ran to the gate, then back to him, still hollering. He followed them through the gate, into the pasture, and down the hill to the well. There, they stood at the well, hollering. The boards covering the well had fallen in, and Tex saw the gander down in the well.

"He got him out, and the geese stopped honking. They've never come to the shop again. Geese have brains!"

Spay! Neuter! Care!

Q Why do I have to spend the money to spay and neuter my cat and dog? It's so expensive!
— J. R.

A It's money well spent, for the sake of your animals' health and also to help the millions of homeless animals in this country.

Many animal shelters and humane societies have low-cost spay-neuter programs.

Also, SPAY/USA is a national dog and cat spay-neuter referral service in several hundred cities. Its volunteers line up veterinarians with excellent surgery and public service records to do low-cost spays and neuters. Its toll-free number is (800) 248-SPAY. This wonderful organization also wants to hear from veterinarians interested in joining.

> "The greatest pleasure of a dog is that you may make a fool of yourself with him and not only will he not scold you, but he will make a fool of himself, too."
> — Samuel Butler

Love Me, Love My Furry Family

Q Ever since we met ten months ago, my boyfriend Larry has griped about my cats, Bruiser and Babe. Now he's given me an ultimatum: Either they go or he does. What should I do?
— Jill R.

> "It is only the law that keeps me from adopting another dozen animals. They are the best, most eccentric, funniest, most affectionate, loyal and highly individual 'people' I know."
> — Ali MacGraw

A Smile at Larry as you whisper those three little words: "Bye bye now."

He has no more right to demand that you give up your beloved companions than to insist you give up a child or a passion for music or any other major part of your life.

Look for a kind person who respects animals—and you! A study by the State University of New York found that couples with animal companions have better relationships, less stress, and healthier hearts than animal-less couples. Spouses with animals interact more closely and have more close friends than those without them.

Truckers' Alert

> *"I care not for a man's religion whose dog and cat are not the better for it."*
> — Abraham Lincoln

Q I found my dog in a ditch in 100-degree heat, licking his legs. He had flown from the back of a pickup truck on a turn, and both front legs were shattered in the accident.

The vet determined from the leg infections and dehydration that he'd been there two weeks.

We found the dog's owner, who spurned him and the vet bills. That's when I renamed this great dog Dudley Do-Right and took him home. He's gained 25 pounds and never leaves my side.

— Kathy

A Pickup drivers, gear down and listen up. Not only can dogs fly from your truck beds, but if you chain them there, they also can hang themselves. From the truck bed, they're forced to suck up exhaust fumes, do the Hot Foot Tango or Frozen Toes Flamenco on the metal and suffer all the weather extremes. This makes you look lower than a snake's belly in a wagon rut. So put your best friend where he belongs—next to you in the cab. There's a good boy.

Animals Do Not Live By Bread Alone

Q The man next door keeps a goat tied up in his backyard. The goat bleats constantly; I know he is lonely. There's a turkey there too. The turkey stands next to the goat, and sometimes the goat licks the top of the turkey's head. I asked the man to get the goat a goat companion and the turkey a turkey companion, but he just laughed and shook his head.

> *"Every day, in countless ways, humans are destroying the relationships of other animals."*
> — Marjorie Spiegel, *The Dreaded Comparison*

— J.D.

A How sad. Please explain to your neighbor that both of these animals have deep psychological needs for others of their own kind. The goat is a herd animal and the turkey is a flock animal. Furthermore, keeping the goat tied is cruel.

How often we deny animals their compelling psychological needs! There's no doubt that many animals whose relationships are destroyed ache with loneliness and grief. When one of two orphaned raccoons I hand-raised disappeared for two days, her brother languished on a high oak branch stub the whole time, gazing down inconsolably when we tried to tempt him with raisins, his favorite treat. When she finally returned, he scrambled to the ground to greet her, chirruping and licking her face.

Other examples abound.
* Four years ago, a donkey attacked his guardian after he sold the donkey's lifelong companion.

* A hippopotamus named Garth broke out of Octagon Wildlife Sanctuary in Florida after his twin brother died. "He was looking for his brother," said Octagon spokeswoman Judy Maupin. "He's just lonely out there at night. He's a big, old, lovable guy."
* One Valentine's Day in France, Pankov, an Asian elephant, died of a broken heart. Pankov had simply stopped eating a month earlier when her mate Mako died. The two had been together for 34 years.
* Three weeks before Pankov died, Kenny, a three-year-old baby Asian elephant with Ringling Bros. and Barnum & Bailey Circus, died after being forced to perform despite the fact that he was sick. In their homelands, baby elephants stay with their mothers at least fifteen years. However, Ringling Bros. took Kenny from his mother without a second thought to break him for the ring.

One morning I arrived at an Illinois wildlife rehabilitation center just as Sally Joosten, its director, drove up. We went in together. She peeked in the bathroom, then became very concerned.

"I left a goose with two taped broken wings in the bathtub last night. He had been shot by a hunter and left to die. A woman found him and brought him in. Now he's gone!" she said.

We searched the Center, a two-story house. Finally, Sally walked over to a tall refrigerator carton, tipped it slightly and peered inside. "Omigosh," she exclaimed. "Will you look at this?" I looked into the carton and there were two geese huddled together at its bottom.

"Even with two broken wings," said Sally, shaking her head in wonder, "he managed to get out of that tub and over the side of this tall box so he could be with one of his own."

DOG AND CAT BREEDERS BREED SUFFERING

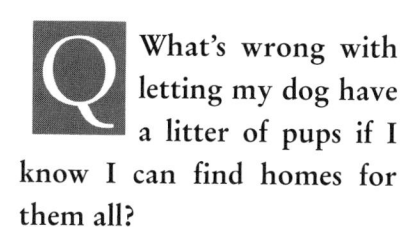

Q What's wrong with letting my dog have a litter of pups if I know I can find homes for them all?

— D.D.

A There aren't enough homes to go around for animals. That's why my hat's off to billionaire John Paul Getty II and his wife, Victoria, who set a wonderful example by adopting a dog from an animal shelter rather than adding to the pet overpopulation problem by buying from a breeder, even though they certainly could afford to buy any breed of dog they wanted without worrying about the price.

> *"For those of us in this movement, the rewards are priceless—no amount of financial success could equal them. The honor of what we're doing makes us feel good about ourselves, our colleagues, our value as human beings, and our lives."*
>
> — Alex Pacheco, PETA co-founder

A member of the Getty household staff picked up the dog, named Bullseye, and drove him to his new life.

"When the driver turned up, we gave him tea." Mrs. Getty told the *Daily Telegraph* reporter. "Bullseye was going crazy in the office next door and left his calling card on the floor."

Because there are millions of homeless dogs and cats in this country, national humane organizations are now promoting local ordinances to curtail their breeding. Dog and cat breeders strongly oppose these ordinances; they want to limit breeding only to the horrible puppy mills that churn out puppies for pet shops and other dog "users" under miserable conditions.

But breeding cats and dogs under even the best conditions when millions of others are homeless is selfish and irresponsible. Every purposely-bred puppy or kitten that gets a home pushes a homeless animal into the euthanasia room. It's that simple.

This fact would come home to breeders if they would volunteer on a regular basis to euthanize the trusting, hopeful animals at their local shelter. That's when looking into a pair of frightened, questioning eyes becomes very personal. I know. I've been there.

For a packet of information on how to get an ordinance passed to curtail breeding in your town, contact The Fund For Animals (see resources page 155).

THE MAGIC OF BIRDS

> *"Flight is an art akin to music, with rhythm and feeling of movement as its foundation, a glorious means of expression that birds, with their emotional natures, know well how to use."*
>
> — Len Howard, *Birds as Individuals*

Q I'm thinking of buying some parakeets and parrots from the pet store here and then releasing them. Would this be okay? I feel that even a few weeks or days of freedom to spread their wings with no restrictions whatsoever would be better than a lifetime of imprisonment in a cage.

— R.T.

A Unfortunately, your idea's impractical. You'd be encouraging the store to replace the birds you bought with more birds.

Also, birds raised in captivity seldom survive in the wild. Not only are they frightened, but also they have a terrible time battling the elements and finding territories, food, and water. There are some colorful flocks of escapees, Amazon parrots, cockatoos, parakeets, and others brightening the landscapes in southern California, Florida, and Hawaii, but they are the hardiest of the hardy; many birds who escape to freedom, even in warm climates, perish.

However, I totally empathize with you. The magic of birds is the magic of flight. It's an incredibly beautiful magic that enchants us humans. So what do we do? We cage birds. We clip their wings. We end the magic.

No doubt I'll ruffle some feathers here, but the best thing you can do is to urge people not to buy birds from stores or private breeders or anywhere else. Instead, they should check shelters, humane societies, animal rights groups, newspapers, and nursing homes—birds often outlive their human companions. Also, an adopted bird should live with one or more companion birds of the same or a compatible species. Check with an avian veterinarian regarding this and the birds' health, and always introduce the birds to each other slowly. And never separate captive birds who have bonded.

If I were an "inside" bird, I'd like to live with Carol and Bill Kath. Carol, a veterinary nurse, has brought home Phoenix, Rosie, and Peeps from the clinic where she works. All were rejected by their owners. Every evening, these birds get to fly inside the Kath condominium. Where do they land? On Carol and Bill's shoulders. When a bird flies to his or her guardian, that's love.

Phoenix is a green and gray Quaker parrot, brought to the clinic to be euthanized because he limps. Rosie is a green-with-orange-cheeks cockatiel, who was rejected because her feet turn sideways. Peeps is a green and orange lovebird whose owner never returned for him.

"They like their routines," says Carol. "Every night, they are let out. If we ever miss a night, they get angry," says Carol. "Then the next night, Phoenix will still be sulking and refuse to come out, and if I reach in, he'll bite me. So we try never to miss a night. When the 11 p.m. news comes on, I say, 'It's time to go to bed,' and they fly to their cages.

"They like fruits and veggies. Phoenix just rips a carrot to shreds. They love zucchini and bananas. Rosie likes grapes. And they all like mashed potatoes. I put a bowlful on the table, and they dig in. Their whole faces are full of mashed potatoes.

"Birds shouldn't be mean, but people handle them, and then they don't. The bird craves attention and he's left alone in his cage. It's solitary confinement, no wonder he gets mean."

Carol stressed the importance of "bird-proofing" a room, so it will be safe to fly in.

For more about this and other bird needs, send for PETA's free fact sheet, Captured or Captive-Bred Birds.

Vaccination Quandaries

> *"Compassion for animals is intimately connected with goodness of character; and it may be confidently asserted that he who is cruel to animals cannot be a good man."*
>
> — Arthur Schopenhauer

Q Last January, my neighbor and I had our cats vaccinated. In February, my Snowy developed a malignant fibrosarcoma at the injection site, which my veterinarian told me was caused by a reaction to the vaccines. Despite surgery, I had to put my beloved Snowy to sleep. Then my neighbor's cat developed cancer and had to be put to sleep too.

I have consulted a number of veterinarians and learned that they're starting to see a trend of cats developing cancers when they receive multiple vaccines, including the feline leukemia vaccine.

— S. S.

A Some veterinarians now think the vaccines in shots given all at one time can overload an animal's immune system, making him or her vulnerable to cancer. A few think that animals who have been vaccinated when they're young are protected for life and don't need yearly boosters, although the law may require them for rabies.

I recommend that people consult with their own veterinarians about vaccine timing and overload.

Incidentally, my own darling dog Nellie developed benign lumps under the skin on the back of her neck, where she had received many injections. Whether the injections had anything to do with this, I do not know.

TRAINING HORSES OR TORTURING THEM?

Q I'm a trainer in a large stable. I see licensed trainers scream at the horses, beat them, and prod them with sticks. They tie the horses' heads down and tie their mouths shut. They deprive them of food.

When the owners are around, these trainers hug and kiss the horses and treat them like babies. If an owner

> "I had forgotten the depth of feeling one could see in horses' eyes. ... Blue was lonely. Blue was horribly lonely and bored."
>
> — Alice Walker, *Living by the Word*

drops by to observe a training session, the trainer makes an excuse, such as, "Oh, I had Star out earlier. Her training went great today."

Shortly, the horses become lame or so unmanageable that they are unrideable and usually end up at the meat market.

— No name please

A Some horse trainers are gentle, while others make the Terminator look like Mickey Mouse.

Many people refuse to send their horses to another barn for training. If the trainer can't come to the property so they can observe the sessions, these people do the training themselves.

When An Animal Is Missing

> *"And I am my brother's keeper,*
> *And I shall fight his fight;*
> *And speak the word for beast and bird*
> *Till the world shall set things right."*
>
> — Edna Wheeler Wilcox

Q Is pet theft a danger?
— J.M.

A Pet thieves are becoming as common as colds throughout the nation. There's a big market for stolen animals. Many laboratories pay $200 to $400 for an animal, and dissection supply companies are always in need of animals. Thieves called "bunchers" steal dogs and sell them at animal auctions to animal dealers who are licensed to sell them to laboratories.

Animal dealers don't even have to go through auctions to get cats; many dealers pay $2 or so per cat brought to them, no questions asked. One dealer in Pennsylvania simply sent a truck to the local supermarket parking lot every Tuesday and paid $2 for every cat brought to the driver. People came with every cat they could get their hands on, including their neighbors' cats.

Don't leave your animal companions unattended in your car or yard, and don't let them run loose in the neighborhood. Make sure they're wearing tags with your name and current address and telephone number.

It's a good idea to have your dog tattooed through the National Dog Registry (Box 116, Woodstock, NY 12498; phone (800) NDR-DOGS). In some states, it's a crime to experiment on an animal with a tattoo.

If your dog or cat disappears:

* Call local police, shelters, and veterinarians. Visit shelters daily, and leave a photograph with the managers. (If you don't have a photo, take one now.) Call the highway department or animal control office to rule out road kills.

* Comb your neighborhood by foot and car. Call the animal's name at a quiet time, and listen for a response.
* Thieves sometimes call and demand ransom for the animal, so answer all phone calls live, or say on your answering tape when you'll be home. (Thieves won't leave a phone number.) Never meet a caller alone; take along a friend or plainclothes police officer.
* Advertise in local publications. Post notices throughout the area with your animal's picture. Offer a reward with "no questions asked."
* Ask local radio stations to broadcast "missing" bulletins.
* Give your newspaper carrier a few dollars to deliver notices with newspapers one day. (This worked for me once when my cat got out and disappeared.)
* Ask mail carriers, delivery people, children, and others in your area to keep a lookout for your animal. Kids know where many animals are. Ask area schools to announce the missing animal over their speaker systems.
* If there are laboratories or animal dealers' kennels in your area, search them as soon as possible. Do not go alone. Police are authorized to search dealers' premises for missing animals. *You can get free lists of the licensed dealers and laboratories in your area from PETA or from the U.S. Department of Agriculture, Animal and Plant Health Inspection Service, Room 756, 6565 Belcrest Rd., Hyattsville, MD 20782 or see their Web site at www.aphis.usda.gov.*

And take heart! One friend of mine found her dog in a neighbor's fenced-in yard after a television psychic told her to look there.

Bunny Huggers

> *"The soul is the same in all living creatures, although the body of each is different."*
>
> — Hippocrates

Q I have a rabbit who kicks his feet at me as if he's angry. Any idea what could be wrong?

— Jeanne L.

A Captive bunnies need much more care than most people realize and can suffer silently in the best of homes. Bright, social animals, they need affection and stimulation and should live in the house, not outdoors, with supervised excursions outside. They often become good friends with four-footed, as well as two-footed, members of the family. Stamping can be a sign of any frustration, including sexual.

I recommend writing to the House Rabbit Society at 1615 Encinal Ave., Alameda, CA 94501. Its newsletter is guaranteed to help you enrich your bunny's life.

Rat Huggers

> *"We forfeit three-fourths of ourselves to be like other people."*
>
> — Arthur Schopenhauer

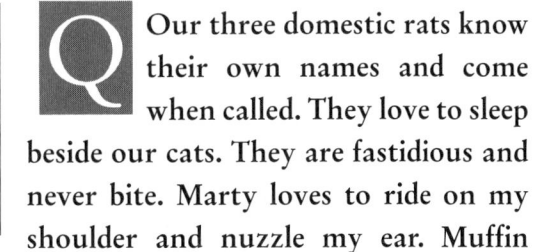

Q Our three domestic rats know their own names and come when called. They love to sleep beside our cats. They are fastidious and never bite. Marty loves to ride on my shoulder and nuzzle my ear. Muffin likes to sleep in the crook of my arm. And Dusty loves to wrestle with my hand. Please tell people that rats are wonderful.

— Erin D.

Our Best Buddies 49

A Domestic rats, descended from wild Norway rats, are to wild rats as dogs are to wolves. Intelligent and social, they are motivated by affection, not food, and bond to people like dogs do. They thrive on kindness and attention and make devoted, playful companions. Their soft tails help them balance and are works of art—the scales on them ruffle back to enable the rat to get a good grip.

Debbie Ducommun publishes the fascinating *Rat Report: The Rat Fan Club Monthly Newsletter*. It's packed with priceless stories and tips about domestic rats. Many Rat Fan Club members have rats rescued from labs or from pet shops where they were being sold for snake food. Domestic rats also are often available at animal shelters.

To find out about subscribing to the Rat Report, send a self-addressed, stamped business envelope to: Rat Fan Club, 1010½ Broadway, Chico, CA 95928.

The PETA contingent of the March for the Animals in Washington, D.C., is led down Pennsylvania Avenue by PETA director of media Dan Mathews and Pretenders' lead singer Chrissie Hynde (both under the "e" and "T" of the PETA banner).

CHAPTER 3

Meals Without Squeals

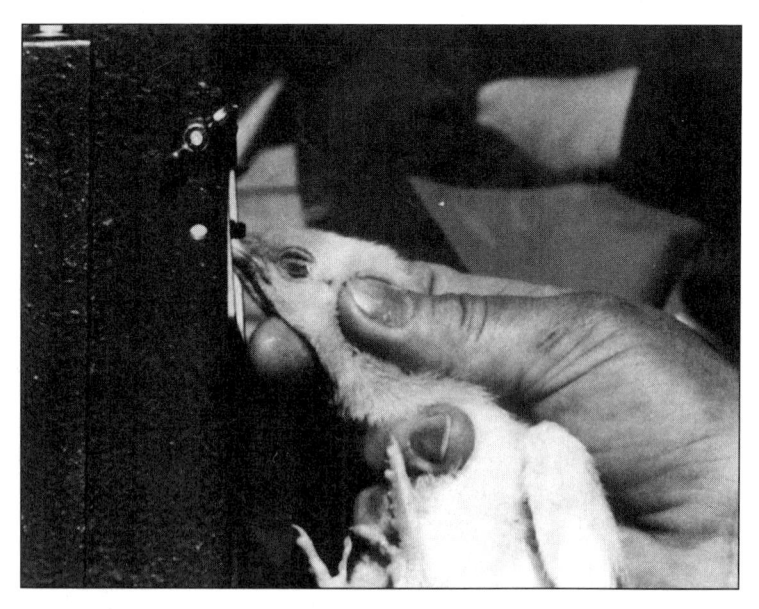

All Baby chicks are routinely debeaked, sometimes losing part of their tongues or tiny faces in the rushed process.

Rich, Famous, and Tender-Hearted

Q What first inspired Paul McCartney and his late wife Linda to become vegetarians?

— Cheri D.

> *"I just don't eat anything that has a mother."*
> — Fred Rogers, *Mister Rogers' Neighborhood*

A The McCartneys lost their taste for meat while watching the lambs frolic on their country estate. From then on, they served only vegetarian food to Paul's band and crew on tours.

People in the arts are known for their sensitivity, so it's not surprising that empathy for animals is the most common reason they go vegetarian. Candice Bergen says she stopped eating animals so she could "look them in the eye." k.d. lang was a vegetarian for years before creating an uproar in the meat industry by doing that infamous "meat stinks" commercial for PETA.

Sara Gilbert flaunted her vegetarianism as Darlene on the *Roseanne* show. Pretenders' lead singer Chrissie Hynde made her no-meat point by flying to Amsterdam to be on hand to thank the McDonald's there when it launched a vegetarian burger.

Linda and Sir Paul McCartney posed for PETA's Merchandise Catalog in their veggie t-shirts.

A few of the many other animal-loving veg-celebs are: Rue McClanahan, Kim Basinger, Alec Baldwin, Kevin Nealon, Sabrina LeBeauf, Sting, Chelsea Clinton, Vladimir Horowitz, Alicia Silverstone, LaToya Jackson, Bill Maher,

52 Living in Harmony with Animals

Michael Jackson, Mary Tyler Moore, Jennie Garth, Cassandra "Elvira" Peterson, Dick Gregory, Bob Barker, David Duchovny, Danny Glover, Brigette Bardot, Cicely Tyson, Woody Harrelson, Gary Shandling, Alice Walker, Grant Alexsander, Sherry Ramsey, Lisa Bonet, Doris Day, Tony LaRussa, and Edward Furlong.

Emmy-award winning actress Rue McClanahan, who works hard for animal rights, filmed public service announcements for PETA with six shelter animals and then adopted them all. Rue is shown with PETA's Teresa Gibbs (left) and Robin Walker (right).

THE RULE OF SEVEN

"I want to apologize for helping to brainwash young people into doing what I now know is wrong—eating burgers and other meat."

— Geoffrey Giuliano, former "Ronald McDonald," now a vegetarian

Q Why is it that my family and close friends seem to be the most dead-set against becoming vegetarian?

— Maria B.

A Maybe a pomegranate frightened them. Be patient. Ingrid Newkirk quotes a study that shows that typically a person is confronted with a new idea seven times before accepting it. After hearing it from, say, a family member, friend, doctor, television show, newspaper, professor—well, you get the gist—the person comes to realize that this is not some crackpot notion, but a concept worth incorporating into his or her lifestyle.

And remember, a letter-to-the-editor you write might be number seven for someone else.

CRUELTY-FREE IS CHOLESTEROL-FREE

Q How does going vegetarian lower my cholesterol?
— Mel R.

> "We don't eat anything that has to be killed for us. We've reached a stage where we really value life."
> — Paul McCartney

A Animal products—meat, eggs, milk, and cheese—are the only foods that contain cholesterol; they also are high in saturated fat, which also raises cholesterol. As for protein, we can get all we need from vegetables and grains. And that old belief that you have to combine certain ones of these to get complete protein no longer stands; all we have to do is eat a reasonable variety of them.

Renowned researcher Dean Ornish, M.D., has proven that a very low-fat, vegetarian diet can actually reverse heart disease.

During my 14 years as a vegan, I've found many simple-to-make dishes. Here are two of my hot-weather favorites.

Audrey Foote's Gazpacho

I never thought I'd like cold soup until Audrey served me this easy, elegant one.

Serves 6

1 medium onion
2 medium tomatoes
1 green bell pepper
1 clove garlic
1 medium cucumber
3 cups vegetable or tomato juice
2 tablespoons red wine vinegar
2 tablespoons lemon juice
1 teaspoon dried tarragon
1 teaspoon fresh basil (½ teaspoon dried)
Pinch ground cumin
Salt and pepper, to taste
2 tablespoons olive oil
Dash hot sauce

Mince the vegetables and then combine all the ingredients. Or, to save time, cube the vegetables and then throw all the ingredients into a blender or food processor, and blend slowly until the vegetables are chunky and the soup is well blended. Chill 2 hours. Serve with Italian or French bread or low-fat nacho chips.

Caroline Woods' Shake

Caroline used to whip up her delicious shakes in the blender in PETA's kitchen and share them with anyone lucky enough to be there at the time.

Serves 2

1 pint blueberries, strawberries, or other fresh or frozen fruit
2 bananas, broken in chunks
½ cup whole almonds (optional)
½ to 1 cup water
Ice cubes (optional)

Put all the ingredients in blender, and liquefy. If the fruit hasn't been chilled, you may want to add a few ice cubes before blending or chill in the fridge before serving.

Variations: You can play around a lot with these shakes. Almost anything goes. In place of almonds, try a dollop of tofu, two tablespoons of wheat germ, ½ cup of bran cereal, or whatever you like. You can add coconut too.

One version of this that PETA people rave about contains 2 bananas, 1 cup vanilla soy milk, and a handful of peanuts. Just blend together and enjoy.

Bon appetít!

Teen Goes Veg

> "I have my message pretty well honed and some are afraid to ask! They don't want to be told about where meat comes from and how it is destroying the planet."
>
> — Actor James Cromwell, who played Farmer Hoggett in the *Babe* movies

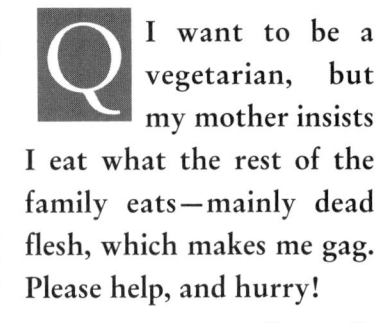

Q I want to be a vegetarian, but my mother insists I eat what the rest of the family eats—mainly dead flesh, which makes me gag. Please help, and hurry!

— Karen B.

A Calm yourself (and your stomach). Remember: Your mom's main concern is your health, so convince her of your nutrition know-how. Eat a variety of whole grains, beans, and fresh fruits and veggies. Get up-to-date info from your local vegetarian society, natural food store, vegan cookbooks, and vegetarian magazines. Share this knowledge with her, and offer to help prepare family meals.

For instance, you might give her the night off from the kitchen and prepare this favorite recipe of Buffalo Bills' head coach Marv Levy, as printed in PETA's *Animal Times* magazine. Serve with potatoes or another vegetable and a salad. Once your family tastes your gourmet grub, they might "veg out" too.

Buffalo Wing-Dings

Serves 6 to 8

2 pounds seitan, cut into strips
3 tablespoons ketchup
2 tablespoons soy sauce
2 teaspoons sugar
¼ teaspoon ground ginger
¼ teaspoon crushed red pepper
¼ cup plus 2 tablespoons water
1 tablespoon cornstarch

In a 12-inch skillet over medium-high heat, brown the seitan on all sides. Add the ketchup, soy sauce, sugar, ginger, crushed red pepper, and ¼ cup water. Heat to boiling. Reduce the heat, cover, and simmer for 5 to 10 minutes.

In a cup, stir the cornstarch with 2 tablespoons water. Gradually stir the cornstarch mixture into the simmering liquid in the skillet. Cook until the mixture boils and thickens slightly.

Pictured left to right—Producers Arnold Shapiro (Rescue 911) and Marie Maxwell Shapiro, actress Rue McClanahan, actor/comedian Kevin Nealon and Linda Nealon got together at Rue's home for a veggie barbeque and screening of "Changing Minds, Changing Times," the video labor of love produced for PETA by the Shapiros and narrated by Candice Bergen.
© *1992 F. P. Denys*

A Pig By Any Other Name Would Be As Sweet

> "I can't look at a pig now without a sense of reverence. I definitely cannot eat, cannot even smell pork now. I actually get queasy if I see someone eat bacon. And I was a big carnivore once."
>
> — George Miller, director of the movie *Babe*

Q Recently I read about a pig named LuLu who saved her mistress's life. Jo Ann Altsman had suffered a heart attack in her bedroom. Witnesses saw LuLu run outside, wait until a car approached, and then walk onto the road and lie down in front of the car. She had never before left the yard, but each time, she pushed open the gate, walked onto the road and laid down and played dead, with all four feet in the air. The first five cars went around her without stopping. Each time a car passed, LuLu ran inside to her mistress, then back outside again. Finally, a car stopped, and a man got out and followed LuLu inside. The doctors said if 15 more minutes had elapsed, Ms. Altsman would have died.

Don't you think we should stop eating pigs?

— J. D.

A Yes, and we should stop beating them too. Many people are concerned about the environmental damage being done by the huge pig factory farms, but they should be even more concerned about the animal misery in these hellholes.

Only because a PETA investigator was able to get on a pig farm and document and videotape the routine horrors is PETA now able to show the world how these animals suffer. Day-to-day abuses included cutting conscious pigs with small scalpels, skinning pigs alive, sawing off two legs of a moaning sow and putting a living sow into the flaming incinerator. Kickings and beatings with crowbars were routine. After beating, stomping, and kicking a collapsed sow, a worker got on top of her and pretended to tap dance.

How can you help these poor animals? First, refuse to buy and eat their bodies. Second, contact your legislators and demand that they stop subsidizing the pork industry.

"Pork producers should be jailed, not bailed out," said Mary Beth Sweetland, PETA's Director of Research, Investigations, and Rescue.

Breeding Tigers

Q I was shocked to read that Thailand wants to breed tigers to slaughter for "medicinal" potions. What is this world coming to?

— J.K

A Its senses, I hope, judging from the mountain of mail PETA received in the wake of this news story. This practice would be as wretched and senseless as the present breeding and slaughtering of more than 160 million sentient beings for their flesh in the United States and Europe each week—that's nearly 23 million animals every day—despite the fact that eating them has been proved to more than double one's risk of cancer and heart disease.

> "Will our tyranny continue, proving that morality counts for nothing when it clashes with self-interest. . . ? Or will we rise to the challenge and prove our capacity for genuine altruism by ending our ruthless exploitation of the species in our power . . . because we recognize that our position is morally indefensible? The way in which we answer this question depends on the way in which each one of us, individually, answers it."
>
> — Peter Singer, *Animal Liberation*

A Horror D'oeuvre

> *"Foie gras is an abomination that every humane individual and organization must reject as a disgrace."*
>
> — Sir John Gielgud

Q I read that Kim Basinger and Alec Baldwin refused to host a Washington, D.C., party until foie gras was removed from the menu. Why?

— M. B.

A Kim and Alec are well aware of the horrors behind foie gras. Foie gras means "fat liver," and is the result of force-feeding ducks or geese huge amounts of food. Three times a day, a worker grabs a bird, holds her down, forces open her bill, and shoves a long metal pipe down her throat all the way to her stomach. The worker then squeezes a lever on the pipe and an air-driven pump blasts two to three pounds of a corn mixture into the bird's stomach. Sometimes an animal explodes.

PETA's undercover investigators' film and photos, taken at Commonwealth Enterprises New York foie gras factory farm, show the pitiful ducks huddled together, pressed against the back of their cages as their torturers approach with the pipes and food buckets. The birds are bedraggled; their eyes are dull and many are unable to walk or stand. Some have broken wings, some have broken legs, some have

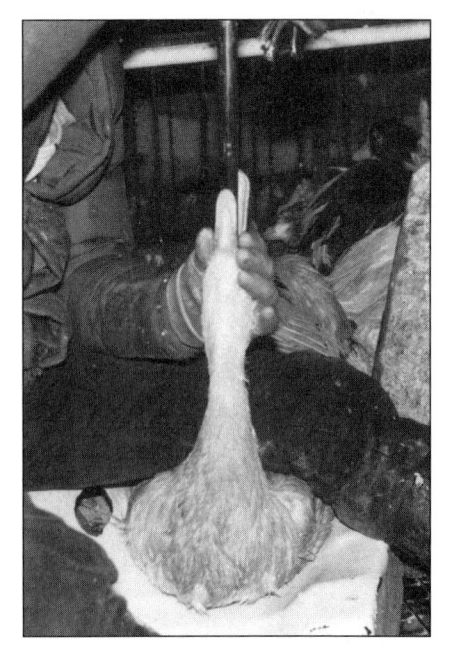

Worker shoving pipe down ducks throat for forced-feeding, photographed by PETA undercover investigator at Commonwealth Enterprises foie gras factory farm in the New York Catskills.

broken bills and some have maggot-infested holes torn through their throats where pipes missed the mark.

When Nobel prize winner and goose expert Konrad Lorenz was asked to read an "expert opinion" of the foie gras industry to the European Parliament, he refused, saying he felt "hot with anger. The `expert opinion'," he said, "is a shame for the whole of Europe."

Promotion of this heinous industry, especially in *The New York Times* and slick culinary magazines, is a shame for the whole of the United States.

Please follow Kim and Alec's lead. When enough people refuse to serve or order foie gras, the demand for it will die and the cruelty will stop.

PETA campaigners Kim Basinger and Alec Baldwin with Eilene Cohhn, PETA director of special events, at The Animals' Ball in Washington, D. C. When Kim and Alec married, they asked friends and family to donate to PETA in lieu of wedding presents. Photo by Terry Adams

A Snorkeler's Awakening

> *"I chose to look full at the steaming kettles in which beautiful voiceless things were being boiled alive."*
>
> — Loren Eiseley, *The Star Thrower*

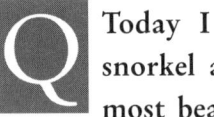

Q Today I was privileged to snorkel among some of the most beautiful sea creatures I've ever seen. When I looked down at my dinner plate this evening at the fried remains of what might have been some of my graceful underwater companions earlier in the day, that did it. I will never eat "seafood" again!

— Don

A Tanks for your post cod, Don. I'm thrilled to the gills over your sea change!

🐾 🐾 🐾

Save Sea Creatures, Save Yourself

> *"They tried to stop me from entering the restaurant kitchen just then, but I pushed past them. There on the counter was a crab, crawling away from a pile of living crabs about to be boiled alive. Like them all, he was covered in batter, even his little eyes. He was trying to escape, even though he couldn't see where he was going."*
>
> — Cam McQueen, Animal activist

Q Don't we need to eat at least fish to stay healthy?

— M. T.

A Absolutely not. Besides, the pollution in water should alarm even the most determined sea animal eater. Since fish, crabs, lobsters, oysters, and other sea creatures literally "breathe" the water they swim in, the U.S. Environmental Protection Agency estimates they absorb up to 9 million times the level of PCBs in that water. They don't eliminate these toxins, but, like all animals, including humans, they accumulate them in their tissues.

Whoever eats them, or the livestock to whom half the world's fish catch is fed, adds these poisons to his or her own tissue warehouse of poisons.

Is it any wonder that we humans, at the top of the food chain, are besieged with cancer?

Save the porpoises, save the fish, save yourself—go vegetarian!

WHAT? TAX MEAT?

Q I've heard that PETA advocates a tax on meat. What could possibly justify such a tax?

— B. B.

> *"Nothing will benefit human health and increase the chances for survival of life on Earth as much as the evolution to a vegetarian diet."*
>
> — Albert Einstein

A Plenty. Meat is rough on human health, our environment, and world hunger. Here are some of the statistics:

* Meat consumption costs Americans an estimated $61 billion each year in health care costs, particularly in the high incidence of heart disease, strokes, and cancer, not to mention E. coli. Since Poland imposed a meat tax, cardiovascular disease there has plummeted nearly 20 percent.

*Animal waste ravages our air, land, and water. The animals imprisoned in today's animal factories never get outside, so their waste has to be dumped. A typical pig factory farm generates ongoing raw waste equivalent to that of a city of 12,000 people. Much animal factory waste is stored in pits a half mile wide and 20 feet deep—massive cesspools of feces and urine that pollute the air and groundwater. Chicken waste is being blamed for the toxic microbe that killed hundreds of thousands of fish in the mid-Atlantic states in 1998. A California dairy factory was indicted for illegally dumping nearly 2 million gallons of cow waste, which flowed into the Amaragosa River and then through Death Valley National Park. Runoff from animal wastes is linked to a 7,000 square-mile "dead zone" in the Gulf of Mexico.

* A vegetarian diet requires 300 gallons of water a day; a carnivorous one, 4,200 gallons a day.
* Forty-five percent of the total land in the United States is used to raise animals for their flesh or crops to feed these animals.
* Twenty pure vegetarians can be fed on the amount of land needed to feed one person consuming a meat-based diet.
* Of all the raw materials and fossil fuels used in the United States, more than one-third go to raise animals for food.
* Rainforests, vital to earth's oxygen supply, are being destroyed at an alarming rate—the top cause is the raising of animals for meat.
* We have permanently lost three-fourths of U.S. topsoil; 85 percent of this loss is directly due to the raising of animals for meat.
* The price of meat would double or triple if the full ecological costs, including fossil fuel use, groundwater depletion, and agriculture chemical pollution, were included in its price.

These statistics have been documented many times over. One of the best books on this subject is John Robbins' Diet for a New America, which was nominated for a Pulitzer Prize.

Taxing meat is not only appropriate; it is imperative.

MEAT: TRUTH IN LABELING

Q I read that the U.S. Department of Agriculture is going to ask consumers for input on labeling meat and poultry. Any suggestions?
— Pete M.

A How about:

"WARNING! SWALLOW AT YOUR OWN RISK. ROTTING FLESH loaded with fat, cholesterol, growth hormones, antibiotics, concentrated pesticides, animal suffering, and ecological devastation. Poultry flesh may also contain cancerous lesions, staphylococci, bleach (to whiten), and/or arsenic. Have telephone numbers of cardiologists and oncologists at hand."

> "A dinner! How horrible! I am to be made the pretext for killing all those wretched animals and birds and fish! Thank you for nothing. Now if it were to be a fast instead of a feast; say a solemn three days' abstention from corpses in my honour, I could at least pretend to believe that it was disinterested. Blood sacrifices are not in my line."
> — George Bernard Shaw, Letter dated Dec. 30, 1929

ACRES AND ACRES OF ANIMALS?

Q If everyone goes vegetarian, what will happen to all the animals?
— L. R.

A Maybe they'll turn into couch potatoes.

> "We all love animals. Why do we call some pets and others 'dinner'?"
> — k.d. lang

When Grammy award-winning superstar k.d. lang teamed up with Lulu the cow to launch PETA's first vegetarian television ad campaign, the press went wild and the cattlemen went ballistic.

Seriously, total vegetarianism won't come overnight. But as more and more people turn vegetarian, the meat moguls will lessen production and gradually shut down their animal factories, just as the furriers are doing now. The relatively few animals remaining will stand more chance of being appreciated for the beautiful individuals they are. Ideally, some might someday evolve back into the magnificent wild beings their ancestors were.

HELP! THERE'S A PIECE OF CALF IN MY MILK!

"One homesick cow walked 30 miles, crossing a river and several highways to return to the Florida farm that sold her."
— From the files of the Humane Society of the United States

Q I heard an animal activist say there's a piece of calf in every dairy product. What did he mean?

— T. T.

A Cows must repeatedly bear calves in order to keep lactating, so the dairy industry spawns the ugly veal calf industry with the babies.

Although a few female calves join the ranks of milk producers, all of the males and most of the female calves are taken from their mothers the day they are born, usually within hours.

Rather than frolicking at his mother's side, as a young animal is meant to do, each calf is chained alone in a veal crate. He is kept immobile so his flesh, when packed as veal, will be non-muscular. He can't even wash himself or turn to bite at flies on his rump. This cruel state of affairs leads to legs weakened so much that many of these adorable animals can no longer stand by the time they go to slaughter. They have to be carried to the truck and thrown onto it.

In addition, they are so weak and vulnerable to infection because of the conditions they're in, that they are routinely fed antibiotics to help prevent disease.

The Joy Of Soy

Q You know, I just can't bring myself to use soymilk. The very name turns me off.

— D. A.

> *"How good it is to be well-fed, healthy, and kind all at the same time."*
>
> — Henry Heimlich, M.D., Sc.D., President of The Heimlich Foundation

A Boy, can I relate to that! I was a vegan for nine whole years before I even tasted soymilk.

I quit drinking milk, but I didn't substitute anything for it. Then one day I tasted a teaspoonful of vanilla soymilk and was so pleasantly surprised I could have kicked myself. Now it's a must on my cereal and in soy shakes. I also use it when I want something in my coffee.

Cow's milk, like poultry and red meat, contains saturated fat, cholesterol, antibiotics, and concentrated pesticides. Organic soymilk contains none of these harmful things. Instead it contains cancer-fighting genistein and is available calcium-enriched.

I urge you to discover the joy of soy. Then page back to "Cruelty-Free is Cholesterol-Free" and try Caroline Wood's Shake (page 55). Yummmm! (And if soymilk still doesn't appeal, try rice milk. It looks more like dairy milk, although it too comes in flavors.)

Wipe Off That Stupid Milk Mustache

> "I no longer recommend dairy products after the age of two years."
> — Benjamin Spock, M.D., *Baby and Child Care*

Q If I quit drinking milk, won't I lose my teeth?
— Walt

A Not if you put them in a glass at night.

Seriously, while milk helps the developing teeth of infant mammals, excessive protein in adults, most often from animal products such as milk, eggs, and meat, can cause an increase in calcium excretion in the urine.

For vegetarians with strong bones and teeth, think horses, moose, and elephants.

If this isn't enough to make you swear off milk, here's a tidbit that might. Consumers Union, publisher of *Consumer Reports* magazine, stated that higher infection rates in cows mean more pus in the milk people drink.

Paula Moore says the dairy industry's slogan should be "Got Pus?"

CALCIUM AND BONE LOSS

Q I'm going through menopause and worried about losing bone density. Don't I need milk?

— C.W.

A No, and Ruth Heidrich, Ph.D., winner of four gold medals in the 60-plus age group of the Senior Olympics, is a perfect example. Diagnosed with breast cancer at 47, she became a vegan that year and started a strenuous exercise program. By the time she reached 60, her bone density had increased from 447 (at age 50) to 466.

> *"Plant-based sources of calcium are plentiful and have advantages over dairy products. Most green leafy vegetables and beans have a form of calcium that is absorbed as well or even a bit better than that in milk. Along with this calcium come vitamins, iron, complex carbohydrates, and fiber, all of which are generally lacking in cow's milk."*
>
> — Neal Barnard, M.D., *Foods That Fight Pain* and *Food for Life*

"This high bone density is despite ingesting no dairy, no calcium supplements, and no estrogen since the onset of menopause," wrote Heidrich. "I repeat, I have a strong family history of osteoporosis, so it's not my genes." Heidrich is the author of *A Race for Life* and *The Race for Life Cookbook* (Hawaii Health Publishers, 1415 Victoria St., #1106, Honolulu, HI 96822).

HOLIDAY DILEMMA

> "If only God had made the animals so they all cried out when they are suffering, it might be a different world. Something so simple could mean so much less agony."
>
> — Alex Pacheco

Q My girlfriend's begging me to go home with her during the holidays, meet her family, and celebrate over a big dead bird. I'm vegan! What should I do?

— G. R.

A Send her parents a card saying you're looking forward to meeting them and that, as you're a vegan, you'll be bringing your most fabulous dish for all to share. (If necessary, practice making the dish before the big day.) If you have no recipes, get free ones from PETA by calling its toll free hotline: (888) VEG-FOOD.

At the table, sit as far away from the corpse as you can, rave over the host's veggie dishes, and be the most charming, nonjudgmental vegan they've ever met. (Have the recipe with you; I bet they'll ask for it.)

WHAT THAT EGG REALLY COSTS

> "Dante could never have dreamed up a hell to equal what human beings inflict on chickens."
>
> — Connie Black

Q Some students stole a chicken from a market as a prank and later brought her to me. Poor Chicken never moved. Then I realized that she was a battery cage hen and couldn't walk. She didn't know how. I had to put food and water within her reach. She had never been given the space to walk even one step—all she had done her whole life was sit in a cage in an egg factory and lay eggs. Then off to a grocery store to be sold live for the pot. She was the most pitiful sight — finally getting her freedom and not being able to move. She never even stood up!

She, of course, didn't make it. My rescued chickens are put to sleep if they are suffering. But Poor Chicken was the saddest of all, because I wasn't able to give her any good years to compensate for her miserable life. She didn't even know how to scratch or peck — she couldn't, because of her machine-severed beak. She existed solely as a kink in a production hose — feed went in one end and twisted into an egg to come out the other.

— Connie B.

A Thanks for the clear picture of why eggs are so cheap. Seems there's nothing more expendable than a chicken.

There are billions of Poor Chickens in the cold hands of corporate America. Buck-eye Eggs is typical. It has 4.6 million hens and is owned by German poultry magnate Anton Pohlman, who was convicted two years ago in Germany of animal cruelty, fined $2 million, and banned from raising chickens in Germany.

At a U. of Baltimore board meeting, surprised poultry magnate Frank purdue takes a tofu pie in his face, delivered on the run by chicken-costumed PETA media manager Jenny Woods. — photo by Peter Wood

In egg factories, as soon as male chicks peck and peep their way out of their shells they are welcomed to the world by being thrown into trash bags to suffocate among their brothers. The female baby chicks are debeaked with a searing wire that sometimes takes part of their tiny tongues or faces in the process. As grown birds, they are packed five hens to a cage the size of a folded newspaper; they can't even stretch a wing. Sores replace feathers as the birds rub against each other. Sometimes their toes literally grow around the wire cage bottom and their feet are torn off when they are pulled from their cages to be trucked to slaughter.

It takes 24 hours in factory farm hell for a hen to produce one egg—one wretched, unhealthy egg.

That Not-So-Studly Steak

> *"It has just stopped me cold from eating another burger."*
> —Oprah Winfrey, after Howard Lyman, ex-dairy rancher-turned-animal activist, told her the always-fatal mad-cow disease could spread to the United States.

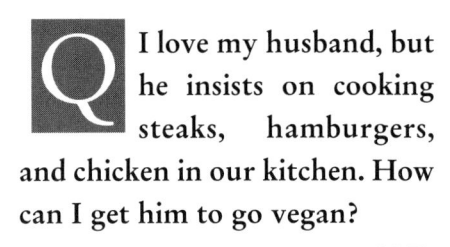

Q I love my husband, but he insists on cooking steaks, hamburgers, and chicken in our kitchen. How can I get him to go vegan?
— M.E.

A I'm sending you a free fact sheet, so you can pepper his flesh dinners with little tidbits like:

"Prostate cancer is 3.6 times higher in men who consume meats, cheese, eggs, and milk daily compared to men who eat few or none of these foods."

or

"You can cut your risk of heart attack by 90 percent by dropping meat, dairy products, and eggs from your diet."

or

"How can you enjoy eating something that might give you mad cow disease?"

Offer to cook or buy him vegetarian meals every other evening, so he can see how varied and delicious they can be.

CHAPTER 4

🐾 🐾 🐾

Shopping
Hitting Corporate Cruelty
Where It Hurts

Cassandra Peterson, alias Elvira, never misses a chance to help the animals. Photo by David Goldner

Fur Is Dead

> "Many years ago, I was in a Broadway show . . . and I had to wear a fox fur around my shoulders. One day my hand touched one of the fox's legs. It seemed to be in two pieces, and I couldn't understand why. Then it dawned on me. Her leg had probably been snapped in two by the steel trap that caught it."
>
> — Bea Arthur

Q I read in our local paper that fur is making a comeback? Is this true?
— Tina M.

A Only in the furriers' dreams. Every so often, especially during the holiday shopping period, newspapers will run articles about how fur is making a comeback. Most—but not all—newspapers are without conscience in their hunger for advertising dollars, including the fur industry's. So they give fur these periodic plugs in hope of breathing life back into this dying industry.

Meanwhile, like any industry in crisis, the furriers are playing the numbers game to boost their sales image. For several years now, they've been including sales of non-fur coats and coats with fur collars or cuffs in their tallies. They even include revenue from fur storage, which is as much as 40 percent of the business some stores do!

As you might suspect, any industry that can inflict such agony on animals also would lie through its teeth and say the animals don't suffer. The statement of Stephanie Kenyon, mouthpiece for the Fur Information Council of America, that "there have been improvements in fur trapping and ranching practices," was directly contradicted by Teresa Platt, executive director of the Fur Commission USA. Platt stated that "chinchillas are electrocuted through a clip attached to the genital area," "neck-breaking when it's done correctly works fine," and, regarding trapped animals, "sometimes a club to the brain renders the animal senseless" and if not dead, it can be shot.

So-called "fur farms" are actually animal concentration camps, where beautiful beings live from babyhood in filthy, barren cages, exposed to the elements so their fur will thicken. Here, they pace and bite the cage wire from birth until death—by neck snapping, hot exhaust fumes, weed-killer injections, or electrocution.

Fur farm owner Lorraine Yurick recently demonstrated electrocution to animal activist Luke Montgomery. Yurick unwittingly allowed Montgomery, posing as a reporter, to videotape her standard anal electrocution of a fox, literally frying the pitiful animal's insides until he died. Later, she stammered, "American people have no problem electrocuting people."

PETA has also documented a fur farmer putting living, screaming chickens, cast off by a pharmaceutical company, feet first into a grinder, to be later fed to his foxes.

By now, almost everyone knows how barbaric the fur industry is, so there's little threat anymore of a fur coat being spray-painted. Instead, the coat speaks for itself—putting it on is like putting on a sign saying, "I support cruelty to animals."

Fur? Grrrrr!

Q Sometimes I feel uncomfortable wearing my fake fur coat for fear people might think it's real. Also, a friend of mine claims fake fur is harder on the environment than real fur. Should I just not wear my fake fur coat?

— Debbie R.

> "The great outdoors is not so great when animals are trapped and beaten to death in it, or raised on fur farms where they are electrocuted or gassed. Fur is something to be ashamed of."
>
> —Tony La Russa, leading an anti-fur demonstration outside the Seattle Fur Exchange

A Just pin a big "NO FUR" button to your coat's lapel and go on your merry way. The buttons are available from PETA and other animal rights organizations. I like to wear one on any coat or jacket; it's such an easy way to make a statement and also has turned out to be a conversation opener amid strangers who are kindred spirits. As PETA's Fur Campaign Coordinator, Peter Wood suggested that we each make such a button a permanent part of our wardrobe.

Fake fur is far kinder to the environment than real fur. It takes 60 times as much energy to make a coat from concentration-camp animals ("ranched" fur) and three times as much energy to make a coat of wild fur as it does to make a fake fur coat.

Raising animals, growing, marketing, and hauling feed for them, driving to traplines, transporting skins to auctions, flying dealers to auctions, and the countless other activities associated with killing beautiful animals for their skins take far more energy than making fake fur coats.

PETA staff writer Karin Bennett (left), the author's daughter, and Lisa Lange, PETA director of public affairs, flank Rocky Raccoon at Gala for the animals.

Don't Let Anyone Pull The Wool Over Your Eyes

Q I'm all for treating animals with compassion, but aren't animal activists stretching it a bit when they say no to wool? This is the kind of thing that makes them sound like their elevator doesn't go to the top floor. The sheep aren't killed, for heaven's sake; they're just sheared.
— LuAnne P.

> *"I've got baaaa-d news for you. Shearers typically have so many animals to wrestle and race thru the shearing line that they get sloppy and slice off chunks of skin—here an ear, there a nose, everywhere the blood flows. If you could see the way ranchers get their woolies, you'd get the willies—believe me.*
>
> *Sport cotton and acrylic instead. Not only are they "kinder" fabrics, you won't be itchin' and stinkin', which are both guaranteed with wool."*
>
> — Karin Bennett

A Trust me, activists don't go looking for cruelty; it's massive in the industries that use animals, and the wool industry is one of the worst. In Australia, where 80 percent of wool is produced, the workers punch holes in the lambs' ears, cut off their tails, castrate the males, and carve huge strips of skin off the backs of the lambs' legs to prevent flystrike—yet the bloody wounds often get flystrike before they heal. And it's all done without anesthesia.

An estimated 1 million sheep die yearly of exposure after premature shearing. Shearers are paid by volume, and one eyewitness stated:

"The shearing shed must be one of the worst places in the world for cruelty to animals. I have seen shearers punch sheep with their shears or fists until the sheep's noses bled. I have seen sheep with half their faces shorn off."

The ultimate horror is the live export of more than 5 million aged sheep yearly from Australia to the Middle East. Tightly packed onto the 14-tier-high ships for the 21-day trip, most cannot even lie down. All are mired in their own waste. Many die. The weak, pitiful survivors are killed in the Middle East by ritual slaughter—having their throats sawed open with knives, often dull. The sheep wave their heads and call out as the blood gushes from their throats. Other sheep are loaded into car trunks for slaughter at buyers' homes.

WALK AWAY FROM LEATHER

> *"Best boots I ever had. Got 'em for $25 at Payless."*
> — k.d. lang

Q Where can I buy non-leather footwear?
— Margie D.

A Genuine non-leather shoes become more in step every day. Actress Sabrina LeBeauf finds them among Kenneth Cole's "Unlisted" line. Call 800-KEN-COLE for a catalog or a store near you that carries this line.

Look for shoes made of leather alternatives at department stores, discount department stores, and in catalogs. Try Heartland Products at 800-441-4692 and Nike at 800-344-NIKE.

Chlorenol (called Hydrolite by Avia and Durabuck by Nike) is a great new material that is perforated for breathability and stretches around the foot with the same "give" as leather. It is machine washable.

These mail-order companies specialize in nonleather clothing and accessories:

Aesop, Inc.
P.O. Box 315
N. Cambridge, MA 02140
www.aesopinc.com

Used Rubber USA
597 Haight St.
San Francisco, CA 94117
415-626-9182

Vegetarian Shoes
12 Gardener St.
Brighton BN1 1UP
England
www.vegetarian-shoes.co.uk
011-441-273-691913

Also check out Ethical Wares' at www.veganvillage.co.uk/ethical-wares, and Vegan Wares at www.webit-designs.com/vegan.

Remember that British shoe sizes usually are one size smaller than North American.

Down With Feathers

Q Why shouldn't I buy down or feathers?

— M. J.

> "Rest? You can rest after you die."
> — Eilene Cohhn, PETA's Special Events Coordinator

A When it comes to animal agony, feathers and down are on a par with fur.

Down is the soft underfeathering commonly plucked out of live geese who are raised for food. Four or five times in their lives, these pitiful birds will feel the painful tearing of these feathers; then, finally, they are sent through a machine that rips out their longest feathers, after which they go to slaughter.

Incidentally, today's cruelty-free synthetic fillers are far superior to down, because they do not lose their insulating ability when wet.

Seeing Is Believing

> *"Life is playing a violin solo in public and learning the instrument as one goes on."*
> — Samuel Butler

Q When I ask a clerk at a cosmetics counter if a product is tested on animals, and she says, "No," how can I be sure she's telling the truth?
— Mindy P.

A Pull PETA's pamphlet from your purse and check for yourself. I carry extras of these little gems, because I find that often cosmetics clerks are interested in them and want one for themselves. Order a supply now—free—from PETA.

By the way, do you know America's favorite detective, Peter Falk, insists that only cruelty-free makeup is used on his *Columbo* and movie sets?

Lookin' Good With Conscience

> *"With more than 500 companies now manufacturing safe, effective products without testing on animals, the tide is turning against the corporate dinosaurs that still do. Don't leave home without PETA's cruelty-free list."*
> — Jason Baker, PETA International Grassroots Campaign Coordinator

Q My boyfriend uses a hair conditioner tested on animals. He claims that no others work for him. He's got this impossible hair—it's real curly and long and gets into one big mat without conditioner. HELP!
— C.L.

A Tell Curlylocks he's all washed up with you unless he switches to John Paul Mitchell's miracle product named, simply, The Conditioner.

Many other companies also make cruelty-free hair care and personal care products. I'm sending you a wallet-sized list of them.

Everyone can get these handy-dandy little pamphlets free from PETA for themselves, their family, and friends. Using them is a great and painless way to help stop animal suffering.

CHEAP, CRUELTY-FREE CLEANING

Q When I read of some big corporation getting fined for dumping toxic waste or some other environmental travesty, I feel quite helpless. What can just one person do to counter such devastation?

— J. R.

> *"We act as though comfort and luxury were the chief components of life, when all that we need to make us happy is something to be enthusiastic about."*
>
> — Charles Kingsley

A Keep the pressure on big polluters to clean up their acts, but also remember that we individuals share the blame with them for poisoning our planet.

I've been rounding up ways to avoid harsh chemicals in everyday living and have come up with the following Earth-friendly cleaning solutions:

* Air Freshener. Leave an open box of baking soda in the room or add cloves and cinnamon to boiling water and simmer. Let the aroma of flowers or herbs drift through your home. Open the windows a while every day. Mmmmm, lovely!

* Camp Cookware. Wash with a baking soda solution or shake baking soda on a damp sponge to remove cooked-on food or grease.
* Copper Cleaner. Use a paste of flour, lemon juice, and salt, or rub salt and vinegar into the copper.
* Drain cleaner. Put ¼ cup of baking soda in a sluggish drain. Follow with ½ cup of vinegar. Close the drain until the fizzing stops; then flush with hot water. I used two teakettles full of boiling water, plus more hot water from the tap. Presto! My drain is now working great!
* Furniture Polish. Mix three parts olive oil with one part vinegar, or one part lemon juice with two parts olive oil. Apply with a soft cloth.
* Headlight, Mirror, Windshield Cleaner. Wipe with a damp cloth or sponge sprinkled with baking soda. Rinse with water and dry with a soft towel.
* Household Cleaner. Three tablespoons baking soda mixed into a quart of warm water
* Linoleum Floor Cleaner. Wash with one cup of white vinegar mixed with 2 gallons of water. Polish with club soda.
* Mildew Remover. Lemon juice or white vinegar and salt.
* Oil and Grease on Driveway. Sprinkle the area with kitty litter, allow it to absorb the oil or grease, then remove it with a shovel or broom.
* Oil Stain Remover. Rub white chalk into the stain before laundering.
* Silver polish. Remove tarnish with a damp sponge or soft cloth dipped in a paste of baking soda and a little water. Rub until clean and buff to a shine.
* Stainless Steel Polish. Use vinegar to remove spots. Shine with baking soda paste (see above) or mineral oil.
* Water Softener. One-fourth cup vinegar in the final rinse. (Also good after shampooing to make hair shine.)
* Wine or Coffee Stains. Blot fresh spill with a cloth soaked with club soda.

CHAPTER 5

Traveling? Take The High Road

PETA's Sue Brebner (left) and Cosby Show star Sabrina LeBeauf (center) hosted a vegan picnic for Washington, D.C., schoolchildren at a sanctuary for rescued animals.

Travel Tips From Linda And Kevin Nealon

> *"But for the sake of some little mouthful of flesh, we deprive a soul of the sun and light, and of that proportion of life and time they had been born to enjoy."*
>
> — Plutarch, *Moralia*

Q Do you have any hints as to how I can keep on my vegetarian diet when I travel?

— Nicole T.

A Even though my mouth is like a convenience store—open 24 hours a day—I've had no problem finding veggie meals when I travel ever since I talked with Linda Nealon, wife of actor/comedian Kevin Nealon. Both are ethical vegans and experts when it comes to eating on the road.

"We pack frozen tofu hot dogs and burgers in our suitcases," said Linda "They're almost thawed when we arrive, and the hotel restaurants store them for us in their refrigerators and prepare them for us later. If we'll have a kitchen, we bring Harvest Direct burger mix and taco mix in foil packs." (For a supply, call (800) 695-2241.)

For restaurants in the United States and Canada, check out the guides published by the Vegetarian Resource Group; (410) 366-8343. In Europe, the Nealons carry *The International Vegetarian Travel Guide*, by The Vegetarian Society U.K. Ltd., Parkdale, Dunham Rd., Altrincham, Cheshire WA14 4QG, and *Europe on 10 Salads a Day*, by Mary Jane and Greg Edwards. (See Resources.) Also, check local phone books for vegetarian and ethnic restaurants.

Here's a favorite Nealon recipe:

Kevin And Linda Nealon's Delicious And Simple Chili

Serves 8

1 tablespoon olive oil
l large onion, diced
½ green bell pepper, chopped
3 (28-ounce) cans crushed tomatoes
2 (40-ounce) cans dark red kidney beans, drained
3 tablespoons chili powder (or to taste)
1 teaspoon salt
1 tablespoon sugar (optional)

Heat the olive oil in a very large frying pan or Dutch oven over medium heat. Add the onion and bell pepper, and sauté until tender, about 5 to 7 minutes. Add all of the remaining ingredients, and bring the mixture to a boil. Lower the heat, cover, and simmer for 1 hour.

● ● ●

FLYING THE UNFRIENDLY SKIES

Q I'm moving to Texas. Which will be less stressful for my dog Luke, flying or driving him?

— Randy M.

A Unless Luke is small enough to fly with you in the passenger cabin, drive him. Flying can be dangerous to an animal's health.

> *"I wouldn't send my cockroach by air."*
> — Phyllis Wright, former Vice President, Humane Society of the United States

Floyd, a golden retriever, had to be euthanized after his brain cooked in a sweltering American Airlines cargo hold. His face and paws were bloody from struggling to get out of his crate.

A judge ruled that Floyd was considered baggage. (However, Floyd's person pursued the case and eventually won a judgement against American.)

Most animals who perish on planes die from lack of oxygen or heatstroke. Sometimes many die on one flight. Fifty-six puppies died on one Trans World Airlines flight, 32 dogs died on one Delta Airlines flight, 24 dogs died on one United Airlines flight, and four dogs died on one American Airlines flight.

Nearly every major airline has been cited and fined repeatedly for violations of the Animal Welfare Act, most resulting in animals' deaths. The U.S. Department of Agriculture doesn't require fatality reports on animals in transit, so no one knows the exact number of animals dying. However, citing airline statistics, Sen. Frank Lautenberg (D-N.J.) said that as many as 500 dogs and cats and 5,000 other animals die each year traveling as airline baggage.

The airlines pay token fines, agree to show training films to their employees, and continue business as usual.

Jim Wippert, a retired Federal Aviation Authority (FAA) Safety Officer, told me that the air flow, and therefore oxygen, to baggage compartments is limited by design to check fires.

"When the oxygen is gone," said Jim, "so is the animal. It happens. My advice for carrying animals in an aircraft is to carry them in the [passenger] cabin."

He said many airline personnel are unaware of this problem. I can attest to this, having been an airline ticket agent for five years; my co-workers and I hadn't a clue. However, airline executives are well aware of the problem. They also know that some personnel throw animal crates around like baggage and when crates break, animals, especially cats, disappear.

Wippert also said animals flying "cargo" usually are brought onto the ramps long before flight time and the high-pitched engine noise and wind, and squeal of the portable power plants drives them crazy. "I've looked into their crates," he says, "and seen their eyes rolling in terror."

By the way, no FAA regulation says an animal can't fly in the cabin with you; an airline can allow this despite its self-written "fit-under-the-seat" rules to the contrary. Movie star Lassie always flew in the cabin.

The moral is, if you can't fly an animal in the cabin, drive him. Should circumstances ever force you to send an animal as cargo:

1) Choose a direct, non-stop flight.
2) Don't ship on a weekend or holiday.
3) Don't ship in severe heat or cold.
4) Ask your veterinarian about tranquilizing the animal.
5) Make sure the kennel is secure, with plenty of ventilation, a ridge around the outside so air holes can't be blocked, and "Live Animal" and "This End Up" printed on its side with arrows and its top.
6) Remove food and water 6 hours before the flight.
7) Give him a *tiny* drink and a brisk walk just before boarding.
8) Make sure the kennel never sits on the ramp long.
9) Upon landing, claim him immediately.
10) Pray a lot.

ANIMALS IN CARS: HOTTER THAN YOU THINK

Q I heard over the supermarket loudspeaker that a dog was overheated inside a car. What do you do if no owner comes out?

— Jesse S.

> "You think these dogs will not be in Heaven? I tell you they will be there long before any of us."
>
> — Robert Louis Stevenson, *Familiar Studies of Men and Books*

A parked car can be as dangerous to an animal as a grooming with a chainsaw. Even with the windows open a bit, a deadly greenhouse effect occurs inside the vehicle. On a 75-degree day, the temperature in a car parked in the sun can hit 120 degrees in 30 minutes; on a 90-degree day, it takes just five minutes. An animal trapped inside can collapse at 110 degrees and die in minutes.

An animal suffering from heat stroke will pant, breathe rapidly, drool, collapse, vomit, convulse, and may even die.

Intervene without hesitation. Enlist bystanders' help. Call 911. If absolutely necessary, get the animal out. (The police can do this too.) Use a belt for a leash.

Soak the animal in cool, but not ice-cold water, then rush him or her to a vet with the car windows open—the lowering of the animal's body heat with moving air is crucial. You can put the air conditioner on too, but keep the animal in the wind (even hot wind) from the windows.

Animal-Friendly Getaways

> *"If someone says 'can't,' that shows you what to do."*
>
> — John Cage

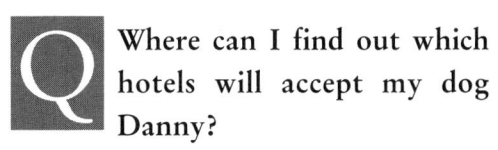

Q Where can I find out which hotels will accept my dog Danny?

— Donna T.

A Taking Danny with you gets easier every day. Just check the Web site: www.petswelcome.com. They list thousands of hotels, motels, inns, and bed and breakfasts throughout the United States, Canada, and France that accept cats, dogs, birds, and other best friends. (Almost all Motel 6s accept them.)

Other unique features include travel and medical tips, emergency pet clinics, a pet bookstore, and Information Xchange to communicate with other pet owners.

Bon voyage!

WEAR TS, SAVE THE SEAS

Q Is it true that suntan lotion is now verboten on some Caribbean beaches?
— David C.

> *"Knowing all truth is less than doing a little bit of good."*
> — Albert Schweitzer

A True as the ocean's blue but turning gray in places. All the oil slicks aren't in Alaska and the Persian Gulf.

Signs have sprouted in the Caribbean, and they'll surely propagate, asking people not to wear suntan lotions into the water. These products harm the sea creatures and delicate coral reefs. The damage is all too apparent in some lagoons, where the water has turned from clear aquamarine to an oily, gray haze. Waterproof suntan oil is better than nonwaterproof, but you can best save your and the fishes' hides by covering up with a T-shirt anywhere you plan to plunge.

Chapter 6

This Is Sport?

Police carry the indomitable Ingrid Newkirk off to jail after she and other protesters disrupted the Hegins, PA., pigeon shoot by running onto the shooting field.

A Psychiatrist Looks At Hunters

Q My cousin goes hunting every chance he gets. He calls himself an ethical hunter, because he eats most of the animals he shoots. What's your opinion?

— Eric D.

> *"When will we reach the point that hunting, the pleasure of killing animals for sport, will be regarded as a mental aberration?*
>
> — Albert Schweitzer

A Let's face it, hunters got into the gene pool when the lifeguard wasn't looking. Dr. Karl Menninger of the renowned Menninger Clinic is quoted in *The Politics of Extinction* as stating that "this joy of killing or inflicting pain" is the product of an "erotic sadistic motivation," and every hunters' book or magazine bears this out.

A good example is actor Kirk Douglas's account of his shooting of a leopard in *Great True Hunts*: "I was aware that when I squeezed the trigger, I had experienced a thrilled surge of emotion that somehow was vaguely familiar . . . the experience left me strangely satisfied, warm, and completely relaxed."

Clinical psychologist Dr. Margaret Brooke-Williams added this insight in the Montgomery Journal, June, 1991: "Most psychologists and psychiatrists concur that what hunters seek subconsciously—and it's nothing to be ashamed of—is reassurance about their sexuality. The feeling of power that hunting brings temporarily alleviates this sexual uneasiness."

In *Use Enough Gun*, Robert Ruark wallowed in the shooting of a hyena: "I shot him nine times with the .220 Swift. I hit him every time, and every time the bullet splattered on his outside. One time I hit him in the face and took away his lower jaw, and still he didn't die. He just bled and began to snap fruitlessly with half a face at his own dragging gut."

True, some children are indoctrinated into hunting by the adults in their family, like my friend Roger, who as a child was taught to hunt, trap, and fish. When he was seven, he killed for the first time. In the woods, all by himself, he came upon a squirrel in one of his traps and made himself stomp the little animal to death. At the time, he got a sick feeling in his stomach. From then on, over the years, each time he killed an animal he got that same sick feeling. But he kept on killing for some time, because he had been taught so thoroughly that this was the thing to do. Then one day he'd finally had enough. He got rid of all his traps, guns, and fishing tackle. With them went the sick feeling, permanently. Today, Roger speaks out against hunting, trapping, and fishing every chance he gets.

The dyed-in-the-wool hunter, like John Corbitt, former editor of *The Mena Star* newspaper in Mena, Ark., lives to kill. Corbitt titled a column, "The joy of killin' stuff," and his opening line was: "I enjoy killin' little furry things." Like so many hunters, he tries to counter criticism by saying it's no different than eating meat from the grocery store.

But eating meat is not the question here. The question is, how can a person take pleasure in killing animals? Because no matter how a hunter tries to justify his murderous pastime, his real reason for hunting is his own cruel amusement.

An ethical hunter? There's no such animal.

Hunting Is Hardly Conservation Of Wildlife

> *"Hunters are a tiny minority, and it's crucial to them that the millions of people who don't hunt not be awakened from their long sleep and become anti-hunting."*
>
> — Joy Williams, "The Killing Game," *Esquire*

Q My husband claims that the killing isn't the main reason he hunts, and also that hunters actually support wildlife in this country. Do they?

— Teresa S.

A Here's an open letter to your husband:

Dear Mr. S.:

If the kill is not the thrill, why don't you carry a camera instead of a gun? You hunters like to portray yourselves as saviors of our forest friends, but blasting their brains out can hardly be called saving them.

Wildlife in this country is controlled not by the 94 percent of us who like animals alive, but by the 6 percent like you, who like to kill them for recreation. This situation has come about because the political action committee of the National Rifle Association, backed by the arms manufacturers, pours money into politicians' campaign funds, and they, when elected, return the favor by naming bloodsportsmen to administer the agencies that oversee our wildlife.

Consequently, you gun nuts swarm through our national and state parks. You've turned 259 of our 452 national wildlife sanctuaries into bloody killing fields. You massacre the animals with semiautomatic rifles, high-powered bows and arrows, and the barbaric steel-jawed leghold trap, outlawed for its cruelty in 70 countries from Argentina to Zimbabwe, but not here—thanks to our wildlife agencies.

You so-called "sportsmen" brag that your license fees and equipment excise taxes pay for wildlife "conservation." But it's our taxes that pay for your "fun"; your money barely pays for the game wardens necessary to police you and the park personnel to pick up your beer cans.

The U.S. Fish and Wildlife Service, state fish and game commissions and departments of natural resources, the U.S. Forest Service, and similar federal and state agencies make all our wildlife laws and use our taxes not to protect wildlife, but for "game management" programs. They only clean up waterways you want to fish. They bulldoze sections of forests and plant low-level vegetation to increase the number of grazing animals—mostly deer—for hunters at the expense of other forest creatures. They allow you to blow away almost all the target species' natural predators. They hand-raise birds such as pheasants, quail, and grouse for tame hunter targets. They transport animals from one state to another to build populations for hunting, and they stimulate breeding with "buck only" hunts, which can leave every buck left alive as many as six does to impregnate.

Then they sound the battle cry: "We must kill them or they will starve!"

You have annihilated almost all cougars, wolves, martens, bobcats, and wolverines. You nearly wiped out bears, and now that they're coming back, you want open season on them again. Two-thirds of our wild duck population is gone, and enough lead shot blankets our wetlands to poison the rest.

You even support the shameful pigeon shoots.

This is how you support the wildlife that "belongs" to all of us.

I urge everyone who's sick of having animal killers call the shots on our wildlife, to speak out on the animals' behalf. Demand that your lawmakers appoint non-hunters to run our wildlife, environmental, and conservation agencies. There are many qualified candidates.

Does Your Favorite Wildlife Charity Support Hunting And Trapping?

> "How does the conservation or animal society you support support you? If it does not, either change it or join one which does. Whatever you decide, do it hard. The hour is late and the animals' need is great."
>
> — Cleveland Amory, *Mankind? Our Incredible War on Wildlife*

Q A friend of ours claims that the National Wildlife Federation actually supports hunting and trapping. Say it isn't so!

— Sue and Don

A It's sad but true. Many "conservation" or "wildlife" organizations support or refuse to take a stand against hunting and trapping for "sport" or "wildlife management."

This Is Sport? 95

Organizations who refuse to take a stand against hunting and trapping include, but are not limited to: the National Wildlife Federation, the National Audubon Society, the Nature Conservancy, the Sierra Club, World Wildlife Fund, the Wildlife Legislative Fund of America, and, of course, federal and state fish and game commissions under various names, such as the U.S. Fish and Wildlife Service, the Department of Conservation, and the infamous Federal Animal Damage Control agency. The Federal Animal Damage Control agency is the cruel arm of the United States Department of Agriculture. It is now trying to whitewash its ruthless past by calling itself Wildlife Services. However, it remains the most relentless wildlife exterminator the United States has ever known.

Alex Pacheco was helicoptered into the wilds of Molokai, where for weeks he and PETA staffer David Barnes scouted for and destroyed more than 700 cruel snare traps set by The Nature Conservancy.

Organizations who stand firmly opposed to hunting and trapping include, but are not limited to: The Fund for Animals, People for the Ethical Treatment of Animals, the World Society for the Protection of Animals, the Association of Veterinarians for Animal Rights, Friends of Animals, the Humane Society of The United States, the Doris Day Animal League, Last Chance for Animals, and In Defense of Animals.

For a more complete list, write PETA.

BONDING OVER BODIES

> "*It's nice to come up on some deer and scare the crap out of 'em.*"
> — Yankee perfect hurler David Wells

Q Do you think it's wholesome for my brother to teach his kids to hunt and trap?
— Mel R.

A About as wholesome as teaching them to shoot heroin.

Consider cases like that of 13-year-old Mitchell Johnson and 11-year-old Andrew Golden. They took the hunting guns belonging to Golden's grandfather, a wildlife conservation officer who had taught Andrew to hunt, and used them to ambush their fellow students in Jonesboro, Ark. The massacre left four little girls and one teacher dead.

Child clinical psychologist and novelist Jonathan Kellerman wrote in *USA Today*: ". . . handing a frightfully immature, troubled human being a firearm and encouraging him to stalk and kill animals is beyond absurd."

Kindness is a learned behavior—kids need to be taught to be kind. And no matter how many Charleton Heston clones spout propaganda that killing is fun and a good thing to do to an animal, it is not. Nor is killing an insignificant part of the hunt, as some hunters claim, a mere by-product of a peaceful day spent communing with nature. Killing the animal is the central thing, the bloody, thrashing, eyes-glazing-over-in-death thing. And it's definitely not kind!

These days, real men are opting for wonderful positive ways to bond outdoors with their kids, such as boating, hiking, climbing, photography, scuba-diving, snorkeling, or any other wholesome adventure that rows one's boat.

Preserve Us From Hunting Preserves

Q What do you think of hunting preserves or "game ranches?"
— Dottie T.

A I did like one game ranch I read about. It was in South Africa. Hunters kept coming and paying money to kill lions. But despite abundant lion tracks, the hunters never had any luck. Then they discovered why. One of them spotted the ranch owner at daybreak padding around with rubber lion paws on his feet.

> "Animals give me more pleasure through the viewfinder of a camera than they ever did in the crosshairs of a gunsight.... I've developed a deep respect for animals. I consider them fellow living creatures with certain rights that should not be violated any more than those of humans."
> — Actor Jimmy Stewart, *The Reader's Digest*

Hunting reaches a new low in game preserves, where people get their kicks killing tame, pen-raised birds or animals.

Lobbyist Tommy Boggs, Jr., made headlines when he and 19 guests at his private Maryland hunting preserve fired a barrage of shots shortly after dawn that killed 182 ducks and left countless others on the ground flopping and bleeding. Even wildlife agents, normally hunters' best friends, were unsettled. They stopped the shoot because the fun-seekers hadn't even bothered to pick up the birds they'd killed, and because they happened to shoot a wild duck.

Yup. One wild duck. The rest were pen-raised, released onto the preserve, knew it as their home, were fed there regularly, and were about as wild as chickens. Thanks to our hunter-run wildlife agencies, there's no bag limit on pen-raised ducks. The naive little birds are as expendable as bubbles in a brewery.

Other people shoot bewildered, scared zoo castoffs game ranch operators purchase at wretched "wild animal" auctions. One ancient black panther, no more wild than my cat Liza, made television news when a bystander at a Texas shooting preserve videotaped gunners poking sticks through the cage into the terrified old guy. He was just lying there, and they were trying to get him to come out so they could shoot him. He eventually stumbled out and these mighty sportsmen executed him.

The tape was run on national television, and viewers were outraged, but the fact is, such activities are business as usual on game preserves. For $5,000, a executive in Detroit can have a panther held in a tree on a Texas game preserve until the executive can hop a plane and shoot the helpless animal.

In Virginia and some other Southeastern states, hunters also patronize bait pens. Here their packs of dogs chase foxes enclosed in areas surrounded by electric fencing. The victims are chased night after night and sooner or later die being ripped apart by dogs—unless it's hunting season, when they may be shot after the dogs run them down and tear into them.

Hunting preserves: Where small men go to feel big.

My Dad The Fisherman

> *"They are sentient organisms, so of course they feel pain."*
> — Dr. Austin Williams, National Marine Fisheries Service zoologist

Q PETA's Anti-Fishing Campaign is embarrassing. I can't talk seriously about cruelty to fish!
— R.P.

A My cod, you needn't flounder when people carp at you about this. Tradition ranks fishing right up there with apple pie and the American flag, but fish are conscious animals who treasure their lives, feel pain, and struggle to survive.

They communicate with sounds inaudible to humans. They use their sensitive tongues, mouths, and lips to gather food, build nests, and sometimes to incubate their eggs. Some show compassion to each other: For a year, one fish in a pet store supported on his back a deformed tankmate, swimming him around the tank and, at feeding time, to the surface.

I've fished myself. My dad was a superb fisherman who often guided others to the best fishing spots in the Northwoods of Wisconsin. He was a gentle man, as are so many fishermen, but he was raised to believe the old tale that "fish are cold-blooded, so they feel no pain." He taught my brother Bob and me to lay a Stanley Weedless or Daredevil down as pretty as you please next to a log in the shallows where a big one might be snoozin' in the sun. Our family cast for muskies, trolled for northerns, fly-fished for trout, and still-fished for walleyes. But I hated to see a fish thrashing on a hook. So I'd go fishing with Dad and hope I wouldn't catch a fish. If I hooked any, I'd hope they were little so I could throw them back. Then I learned that most fish thrown back die later. That's when I abandoned my rod and reel.

Some years later, when my dad caught a huge muskie and held him up for others to see, he got a sad smile on his face. "I feel sorry for him," he said, with embarrassment. Not long after that, he put away his tackle for good.

Today, like most people, my brother and I find pleasure in harmless sports, he in golf and I in swimming.

Fishing also kills millions of small beings used for bait, and other animals as well. One PETA member saw an angler cutting his line after a seabird swallowed the bait. Leaving the hook in the bird's throat, he cursed that this was "the second time this happened to me today."

Driving through Melbourne, Fla., I came upon a sight from hell. A big dead pelican, wings outspread as if in a plea for mercy, dangled from a length of fishline, one end tangled around a telephone wire, the other attached to a hook pulling his guts out through his gaping bill.

How he had suffered! But did he suffer any more than a hooked fish?

A Trapper's Opinion Of Dominion

> "Cruelty is the vice most natural to dullness of mind."
>
> — H.W. Nevinson, *Essays in Freedom and Rebellion*

Q God gave us dominion over the animals. This means He put them here for us to use as we please. Understand?
—Big Ed the trapper

A If God has dominion over us humans, would you rather have Him trapping and stomping us to death for coats or loving and helping us?

Taking center stage in a surprise disruption of an Oscar de la Renta fur show are (left to right) Jenny Woods of PETA, Jane Wiedlin of the Go Go's, and Dan Mathews and Ann Chynowth of PETA. Photo by Ebet Rogers

CHAPTER 7

🐾 🐾 🐾

No Fun For The Animals

Longtime civil rights activist and comedian Dick Gregory spoke out against animal slavery in circuses and other traveling shows, saying these animals "represent the domination and oppression we have fought against for so long." Photo by Tal Ronnen

Backstage At The Big Top

> *"With only two weeks to get ready for opening night at the circus, we had to work fast to get the elephants ready to perform. Sadie, the youngest, was very timid and frightened. One day we had her in the ring for training. She could not do her tricks and ran out of the ring, afraid of punishment. We caught her, brought her back, forced her to the ground, and began to punish her for being so stupid. Suddenly, we stopped hitting her and looked at each other. Sadie was crying like a human being. She lay there on her side, tears streaming down her face and sobs racking her body."*
>
> — George Lewis, *Elephant Tramp*

Q I know some circuses are sleazy and treat the animals cruelly, but what about Ringling Bros. and Barnum & Bailey?

— L. J.

A Ringling Bros. and Barnum & Bailey Circus veterinarian Richard Houck said in a *Greensboro* (N.C.) *News & Record* article dated Feb. 14, 1995, that, when people say the animals are abused, "it really hurts my feelings."

Boo-hoo.

Tell that to the Ringling horse who dropped to the pavement and died after 20 minutes of suffering. It happened Feb. 22, 1999, as Ringling marched its animals from the boxcars to the Scope arena in Norfolk, Va. PETA staffer Tal Ronnen caught the tragic scene on video, and, with other witnesses, heard the Ringling people repeatedly ask the police where they could get a veterinarian. However, the next day on television, Ringling lied, saying that a veterinarian travels with them 24 hours a day.

Tell that to Kenny, the baby elephant who died hours after Ringling forced him to perform while he was sick. Even though elephants in the wild stay with their mothers until they are 15 years old, Ringling took Kenny from his mother at age two and sent him on the boxcar circuit.

Tell that to the caged tiger into whom a Ringling trainer pumped five shotgun blasts after the tiger attacked another trainer earlier that day.

Tell that to the small, screaming Asian elephant caught on videotape as a Ringling trainer whipped her in the face and gouged her with a bull hook.

After watching animals being unloaded from the Ringling Brothers boxcars on March 23, 1989, the Washington, D.C. Humane Society pleaded with the public not to attend the Ringling Brothers Circus. The plea stated that humane officers saw animals frantic for food and water; elephants with scarred skin and open sores; and several handlers using their elephant hooks to repeatedly and forcefully beat elephants who merely were walking in line. Things haven't changed since then.

Previous Ringling owner Henry Ringling North wrote in his book *The Circus Kings*: "All sorts of other brutalities are used to force them to respect the trainers and learn their tricks. They work from fear."

Ringling Bros. is as bad as any other circus. Maybe worse.

Animals in circuses have no privacy, mental stimulation, or physical exercise. Those who naturally roam in family groups or pairs are penned solitarily. In the ring, the whips, tight collars, muzzles, and electric prods remind us that these wild animals are being forced to go against their nature and do senseless "tricks."

To "break" a juvenile elephant, her captors chain her for as long as a month, immobile and legs akimbo, to the ground, and beat her head. Grown elephants also are disciplined by being chained and beaten, but never in public view, of course.

An elephant's skin is super-sensitive; those sharp bull hooks hurt and tear it! More than one elephant has lost an eye to a bull hook. As zookeeper Paul Hunter said, "They are trying to turn these elephants into circus performers. You have to motivate them, and the way you do that is by beating the hell out of them."

After hauling them for years in unventilated railroad cars, freezing in winter and sweltering in summer, circuses often dump spent animals at roadside zoos or exotic animal auctions, which sell them to hunting

Tyke broke out of a circus arena and fled down this Hawaiian street. The police had to pump nearly 100 bullets into the terrified elephant to kill her.

ranches to be shot as "trophies." Others are killed for their meat and/or hides or sold to laboratories for experiments.

Please attend only circuses that don't use animals, such as Cirque du Soleil, Circus Oz from Australia, Circus Vargas, and the Cirque d'Hiver. Ask your friends to do the same. By boycotting animal acts, we can make them history.

Rinky-Dink Roadshow

> "A lesson in standing up for your convictions goes a lot farther than a pony ride."
>
> — Carol Reinhard

Q Mom and I went to the Kelly Miller Circus in our town. The elephant giving people rides all day looked so tired. Whenever the elephant slowed down, the trainer hit her with a long pole with a sharp hook on the end, and she cried "Ow!" Her ears had cuts on them.

The horses' heads were tied down so far they had trouble breathing. When they didn't jump high enough, a man hit them hard. What can we do?

— Pammy Jo D.

A These people are as pleasant as poison ivy. That pole, called a bull hook, hurts and tears the elephant's sensitive skin.

You spotted the cruelty that goes on right in public. Behind the scenes, it is far worse.

In circuses large and small, when the animals aren't performing, which is approximately 98 percent of the time, their long, miserable lives consist of cages, chains, boxcars, thirst, and often beatings.

The good news is that India, Finland, parts of Great Britain, Sweden, Switzerland, Tacoma Park, Md., and Hollywood and Lauderdale Lakes, Fla., have banned exotic animal acts, and, in the future, more towns will surely follow their lead.

I'm sending you information to show your mom about how to go about getting such a ban passed in your town. This information is available free to anyone who calls or writes PETA.

CRUELTY FOR BIG BUCKS

Q To me, rodeos seem cruel to the animals. But my cousin, who lives in Denver, says they're not. Are rodeos cruel?

— T. D.

"Ever occur to you why some of us can be this much concerned with animals suffering? Because government is not. Why not? Animals don't vote."

—- Paul Harvey

A Rodeos are flagrant animal abuse now being presented from coast to coast and on television as all-American entertainment.

In fact, I have right here on my desk an article from the *Denver Post* telling how two horses died last week in the National Western Stock Show and Rodeo there.

One slammed into a wall headfirst, and one bucked so hard that he broke his back.

Shoving electric prods into animals, twisting their necks, yanking them by their necks or legs, and slamming them to the ground and doing all sorts of mean things to make them buck hurts them terribly. However, many of the injuries are internal. C. G. Haber, a veterinarian who worked 30 years as a meat inspector in slaughterhouses, saw scores of animals discarded from rodeos and sent to slaughter. Toughened as he was to animal suffering, the condition of the rodeos' animals sickened him. He described them as "so extensively bruised that the only areas in which the skin was attached to the flesh were the head, neck, legs, and belly.

"I have seen animals," he said, "with six to eight ribs broken from the spine and at times puncturing the lungs. I have seen as much as two to three gallons of free blood accumulated under the detached skin. Bullfights are merciful compared to rodeos. It's high time this cruel sport be outlawed in the United States."

Every major animal protection organization in the United States concurs with him.

This is why, try as it will, the Professional Rodeo Cowboys Association (PRCA) cannot get one national humane organization to support it. Instead, it relies on paid veterinarian shills, not even worthy of the title "veterinarian."

This is why corporate rodeo sponsors refer complaints you make about rodeos to the PRCA, an organization which purports to regulate some 700 rodeos a year. The PRCA then sends you a personalized computer letter and a booklet of "humane rules" that are as worthless as hats in hurricanes. The letter assures you that the animals are treated well because they are valuable and the cowboys hold them in high regard.

Calf roping is the most criticized rodeo act, so to quiet the criticism, the PRCA dreamed up another "humane rule," the "jerk-down" rule. It fines rodeo cowboys if they "jerk down" a calf, that is, slam him or her to the ground. The hypocrisy of this rule was even too much for one of their own. To his credit, here's what Bob Gonzales, PRCA gold card member and rodeo judge for 28 years, wrote about the jerk-down rule in a letter to the Pueblo (Colo.) *Chieftain* newspaper:

"I have seen many, many calves injured or killed . . . These baby calves are not old enough to be weaned and should still be on their mothers . . . All this rule does is give the PRCA more money to vote themselves a raise by fining the cowboy. The only rule that would work for a jerked-down calf would be to disqualify the cowboy or suspend him from competing. . . . I'm sure a cowboy would be glad to jerk a calf down and pay a $100 fine if it meant winning."

Actually, rodeo animals are as available as cuss words around a corral and treated with about as much care. They are not the tough, colorful mavericks rodeo promoters and announcers portray them to be. They are tame, frightened domestic cows and horses tormented into action on this detour to the slaughterhouse. They are cheap and easily replaceable.

But the amount of points a cowboy racks up depends largely upon how wildly his animal behaves, so moments before the chute gates open, rodeo hands prod, goad, and whip the helpless animals into frenzies in the chutes, out of sight of audiences. PRCA Rule 6 states that: "Standard electric prods shall be used as little as possible. Animal shall be touched only on the hip or shoulder area with prod." But the electric prod or "hot shot" is one of the rodeo peoples' favorite and most versatile tools and can draw blood. Even one with only two batteries initially delivers a voltage exceeding 8,000 volts!

Aware of the controversy over their use, stockhands discreetly cover the prods with black friction or electrician's tape to keep the chrome from glinting in the lights or sun. They then conceal them in coats, hip pockets, under shirtsleeves and behind chute boards. A new, more compact prod, little bigger than a hand, is becoming popular.

Despite rodeo hands' attempts to hide their cruelty, humane organizations' files are filled with eyewitness accounts like these:

"A riding bull went down on his knees in the chute and a cowboy was throwing sand into his eyes to get him to stand up."

"The first horse came out of the chute, slammed into the metal grandstand head first, fell to his knees, reeled around, and crashed into the stands again. 'Look at that outlaw go!' whooped the announcer."

Performers aren't the only ones who hurt the animals. In September 1990, one woman sent PETA this account of how violence begets violence:

"I was appalled at the condition of some of the animals at the annual Shriners Rodeo in Wilmington, Mass. During the calf-roping event, a panicked calf in a metal pen, waiting to be roped, tried to climb the metal rails of the pen to get out. A drunk Shriner, funny hat and all, ran over and repeatedly punched the calf in the face until the calf fell to the ground."

One can imagine the terror of animals like this poor calf, including the steers, bulls, and horses, who are equally innocent and bewildered. They spent hours or days just trying to keep their balance during a hot, bumpy truck ride, jammed in among other frightened animals, to the rodeo grounds. Then, tired and thirsty, they are jerked around and shoved into a chute and hot-shotted and prodded to make them bolt into an arena surrounded by a bellowing crowd.

The woman also complained that in the bucking bronco event at this same Shriners' rodeo, "one horse was used so much" that when the bucking strap was removed, "his fur was all worn off, and he had a red welt all the way around his belly."

Another person wrote to complain about the DuPage County Fair in Wheaton, Ill.: ". . . 100-degree weather and the horses had no water. Despite my complaints to owners, fair officials, and police, nothing was done. These horses were also covered with cuts and whip marks. Many were bleeding. No hay was provided. The manure was ankle-deep."

Although much of the abuse is right before rodeo viewers' eyes, many of them like to think that animals like those they eat are insensitive to pain. But just like other animals, including humans, these animals are capable of feeling extreme pain and fear. Consider how a steer will flick away a biting fly with his tail; then compare this with the pain of a spur ripping into his shoulder or his body being slammed to the ground.

Promoters also capitalize on the fact that many of the animals' injuries are internal and the animals can be quickly pulled from the arena as the announcer assures the audience that "Ol' Duke's just fine, folks, he just had the wind knocked out of him."

Because all the national humane groups are against rodeo, the best supportive opinions the PRCA can come up with for its booklets are from veterinarians in its own ranks. This one, from Ohio State animal researcher Albert Gabel, appears in a PRCA booklet titled, "No Room for Cruelty": "I'm an old farm boy, and rodeo is very well within my guidelines of how animals can be useful to humans." More proof that a veterinary degree is no more proof of humaneness than a fat wallet is of integrity is T. K. Hardy, a Texas veterinarian and sometime steer-roper who told *Newsweek*: "I keep 30 head of cattle around for practice at $200 a head. You can cripple three or four in an afternoon."

With friends like these, what animals need enemies?

A PETA member lives in western cattle country. Her neighbor, a past PRCA participant, raises calves for rodeos.

"The little calves," she says, "were a delight to watch, frolicking in the warm spring sunshine, playing tag and chasing each other and kicking their heels high in the air, enjoying their beautiful habitat.

"Then one day when I drove by," she continues, "I saw this gathering of pickup trucks and horse trailers by the calves' pasture. There were these big men practicing for the rodeo, with `chawin' tobaccy' in their jaws, swinging their lariats overhead, pounding their own saddle mounts' rumps, and yellin' hyaaahhh!' at these little quarter-grown calves, who were startled half to death.

"The next day when I passed by again, my heart sank. There were these poor spirit-broken animals limping along the fence line, heads and ears down, trying to get into comfortable positions after their day of torture at the hands of the very people who had previously fed them and tended to their needs. What trauma!"

Sadly, the worst was yet to come for these animals.

Happily, we can help, simply by staying away from rodeos and asking others to do the same.

Ridin', Ropin', and Regrettin'

> "If that big brave rodeo cowboy would relinquish his bucking strap, electric prod, and spurs, he would not only be out of business, but we would have a chance to see him for what he really is—someone who, in my opinion, needs prolonged psychiatric treatment."
>
> —Amy Freeman Lee, *On the Fifth Day*

Q Rodeos are so disgusting. I saw a rodeo with so-called cowboys wrestling steers, only what they call steers are really calves. Those rodeo men were such bullies! They seem to think that treating animals so roughly makes them appear tough and manly. It's the opposite of being a horse whisperer—now there's the kind of man I can respect.

— Donna T.

A And image isn't all these guys have to worry about. Here's what Irwin Goldstein, M.D., urologist at the Boston University School of Medicine, had to say in a Jan. 17, 1995, Canadian Broadcasting Corporation interview:

"The reality of the anatomy of a man's crotch is that the artery that sends the high-pressured fluid-flow to the penis during sexual stimulation passes underneath the pelvic bone . . . so a crushing blow . . . can, unfortunately, impair and occlude the plumbing hose to the penis, so that it is the equivalent of the penis having a heart attack, if you like, so that with sexual stimulation, not enough high-pressured blood enters the penis, and impotence results. . . . When you sit on the horse, you're sitting on the base of the penis, period. I would venture to say that most rodeo riders have erection problems."

Are you listening, fellas?

For more on rodeos, please keep reading.

Charreadas And One Happy Ending

Q I was shocked to see a television documentary about charreadas, Mexican rodeos, being held in the southwestern United States. Men whip frightened horses to make them run around an enclosure and lasso their front legs as they run. The horses trip and break their legs or necks or even backs. The film showed the broken horses lying in the hot sun for hours before they're dragged off to the slaughterhouse. It was horrible!

> *"And I thought, yes, the animals are forced to become for us merely 'images' of what they once so beautifully expressed."*
> —Alice Walker, "Am I Blue" *Living by the Word*

— T. R.

A Charreadas are being staged surreptitiously in remote fields in southwestern states. Often armed guards are present and conduct full body searches for weapons and cameras. These rodeos will grow in number until states enact strict laws against them.

People in California and New Mexico should be proud that their states have made charreadas illegal.

Here's the story of one horse saved from a charreada:

Sarah Owen of California once trained to be a jockey but quit when she saw how badly many racehorses are treated. Often the horses break under the pressure of racing and are sold to rodeos or slaughterhouses. Since corporations today own most racehorses, few people care what happens to them after they are discarded.

"Jet Frost was a two-year-old, just a baby," says Sarah. "Because her nature was so sensitive and gentle, she couldn't handle the stress of racing. She had a nervous breakdown. She refused to run, refused to eat, just stood with her head in the corner of her stall, weaving back and forth like an abused child."

She began to try to attack any man who entered her stall. Nevertheless, her handlers would yank her out, throw a saddle on her, and force her to run. Regardless of how a horse feels physically or mentally, she must be forced to run.

The corporation wasn't interested in nurturing Jet Frost and arranged to sell her to a charreada. But during the night preceding the day she was to be trucked away, Sarah got a call from a stablehand about this horse "colicking and in great pain."

"I bought her and brought her home," said Sarah. "I let her just play and have her freedom for eight months. She got very attached to me. When she saw my car drive up, she ran to the fence and I petted her. She became very playful.

"Now her favorite game is: She gallops off in one direction and I run the opposite way. Suddenly she turns and races full blast straight at me— I huddle on the ground, my arms around my head, and just as this ton of horse is about to trample me, she stops on a dime and nuzzles my arm.

"This sweet, glorious horse and I have had a wonderful friendship for the last 10 years."

Sarah said Jet Frost and Zack, another horse rescuee, are madly in love. They are inseparable.

"Some days," she said, "I'll ride Zack far into the hills, leading Jet Frost alongside. Then I take her halter off and let her run free. Before going home, I switch horses and let Zack run free. Most horses never get this freedom to stretch and run at will.

"And after all, that's what they're meant to do. Just like birds are born to soar, horses are born to run free."

THE BAD NEWS ABOUT ZOOS

Q Although the zoo in our city is clean and the animals are well fed, I still get a sinking feeling when I look at the animals there behind the bars. Do you think zoos that save endangered species are worthwhile?
— A.R.

A Your gut instinct is right: Zoos are basically bad news for the animals. I recommend that anyone hankering to see some animals steer clear of the zoo and, instead, visit a non-profit sanctuary that rescues homeless, exotic animals or volunteer at a wildlife rehabilitation center. Also, my daughter Kris and her friend Lorie find it fun and good exercise to volunteer to walk some of the dogs at their local animal shelter.

Zoos take animals from their homelands and families or breed them and take them from their mothers to put on display.

Zoos claim they preserve endangered species, but a 1994 report by the Born Free Foundation (BFF) revealed that only 2 percent of the world's threatened or endangered species are registered in breeding programs. Mostly, zoos breed animals with no intentions of keeping them, so they can have a constant supply of those cute baby animals that draw in the public in droves. Every year, former babies, now grown, are sold or given away to dealers in the huge exotic species marketplace, which sell many animals to shabby roadside zoos or to hunting ranches to be shot as trophies.

> *"I have empathy for wild animals incarcerated against their will, whether it is in a circus, a zoo, or a 'safari park.' Who wouldn't rather be free to do the things they love under their own power, on their own time? It doesn't take a lot of imagination to look at a dispirited, leg-shackled elephant staked out behind the big top to see the look of a slave reflected in those eyes."*
>
> — Richard Pryor

Debra Jordan, former zoo nursery director, tells how management ordered her to display baby animals and tell the public their mothers abandoned them. "The truth was," she states, "that the animals were either pulled from their parents or intentionally bred to be placed in the nursery's display windows."

A two-year investigation reported by the *San Jose Mercury News* revealed that 19,361 mammals left zoos from 1992 through mid-1998. Of those, 38 percent went to hunting ranches, animal auctions, dealers, unaccredited zoos, game farms, or unidentified individuals. More than 5,200 of the animals went to dealers, and from there it is unclear what happened to them. Dealers sell to many places, including hunting ranches and laboratories. According to the report, the zoos that sent the largest number of animals to dealers included the renowned San Diego Zoo and the San Diego Wild Animal Park.

Kristin Bennett, the author's daughter, helps out at the local animal shelter every week by walking the dogs there. Photo by Lorie Rienstra

Sometimes you'll see a monkey making the same movements over and over, like the white mangay in a Paris zoo who endlessly flipped around her cage. Other animals manifest zoochosis—animal insanity—by constantly biting or licking cage bars or walls, neck rolling, vomiting and eating the vomit, walking in circles, placing footsteps in the same places, playing with and eating excrement, head-bobbing, swaying and self-mutilation, including hair-plucking, tail-biting, head-banging, etc. Almost every zoo visitor has witnessed some of these zoochoses, but many fail to realize that they signal an animal literally going crazy in captivity.

Zoos control animals by force. During the transportation of Dunda, an elephant, to the San Diego Wild Animal Park, her tranquilizer wore off, leaving her frightened to find herself in a strange environment with all four legs chained. She began to struggle. For two days, shocked passersby saw keepers beat her head with ax handles, elephant hooks, and shovels.

Said Saul Kitchener, director of the San Francisco Zoological Gardens, "How do you get a 10,000-pound elephant's attention? Hit him, that's how."

Incredibly, zoos sell meat in zoo snack shops and fail to promote vegetarianism. Yet half of all species on Earth live in the tropical rain forests, which the meat industry is eradicating faster than you can say "two all-beef patties" in order to graze cattle to export to the United States. In 1960, Central America had 130,000 square miles of virgin rain forests; today, fewer than 80,000 square miles remain. At this rate, in 40 more years, these priceless ecosystems and their animals will be history. The flesh industry has also destroyed 260 million acres of U.S. forests to graze cattle and raise feed for them. If we stopped raising crops to process through livestock and instead fed the crops directly to people, we could turn 200 million U.S. acres back into forest habitat. But rain forests, once gone, are irretrievable.

We don't need zoos. We can support the non-profit sanctuaries that rescue and care for exotic animals but don't sell or breed them. We can establish environmental education centers and rehabilitation facilities for native animals. Let people volunteer to help these local animals and thereby develop a better appreciation for them.

I did. At a visit to a wildlife rehabilitation facility, I mixed baby animal formula and watched a volunteer dentist check a sedated woodchuck's incisors—they had been broken off at the gums in a car encounter but were growing back beautifully. All the while, a Canada goose wearing a wing splint wandered about, stretching his long black neck to peer into the other patients' cages.

Here, all the animals' eyes shone with spirit—there wasn't a glazed stare or zoochosis in the place. I swear these animals knew we had their best interests at heart.

At a well-run sanctuary like this, you don't get a sinking feeling. You feel great.

The Day Willie B. Kissed A Tree

> *"Men have forgotten this truth, but you must not forget it. You remain responsible forever for what you have tamed.*
> — Antoine de Saint-Exupery, *The Little Prince*

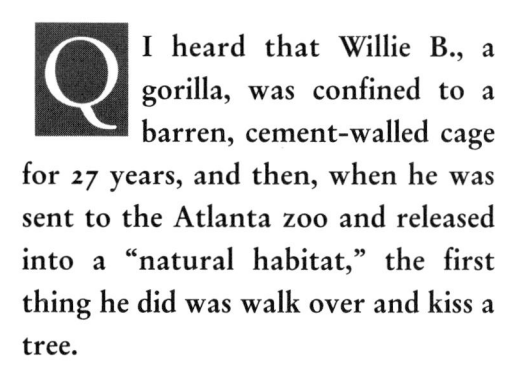

Q I heard that Willie B., a gorilla, was confined to a barren, cement-walled cage for 27 years, and then, when he was sent to the Atlanta zoo and released into a "natural habitat," the first thing he did was walk over and kiss a tree.

— K. T.

A Yes, it's true. Isn't it a poignant example of how things we take for granted mean so much to animals deprived of them?

The Lure Of Aquariums: Don't Bite

Q My boy friend Sam says marine aquariums are good, that they educate people about whales and dolphins and other sea life. I say leave sea creatures in the sea. Who buys dinner?
—M. M.

> *"It is nothing short of torture to take these animals—who are accustomed to the infinite beauty of the open seas, covering vast distances at speeds sometimes reaching 60 kilometers an hour—and then imprison them in tiny concrete or metal pools."*
> —Professor G. Pilleri

A Aquariums are wet zoos and are poor substitutes for the sea creatures' natural surroundings and homes.

Ask Sam how he'd like living in a closet with 20 blaring radios tuned to different stations.

In the seas, dolphins and other whales define their realm acoustically and communicate over hundreds of miles. In tanks, they are barraged with garbles of sounds that may drive them crazy.

In the sea, these highly sensitive and intelligent mammals live in pods and have strong bonds with each other and strong senses of their own identity. Free dolphins live an average of 45 years, but in captivity, half die after two years.

Jean-Michel Cousteau, son of the late marine explorer Jacques Cousteau, told of one dolphin who, after several weeks of captivity, committed suicide by ramming his head into the side of the tank. Said Jean-Michel Cousteau: "The display of marine mammals for commercial gain does not represent the values we should be passing on to future generations. By what right do we presume to deprive these creatures of their freedom and starve them into performing trivial feats for our diversion? We are not gods with a self-bestowed mandate to treat other species as exploitable resources. Rather, we owe these magnificent fellow travelers the right of way in their own domain."

Bullfights: Tradition of Torture

> "The awful wrongs and sufferings forced upon the innocent, helpless, faithful animal race form the blackest chapter in the whole world history."
>
> —Edward Augustus Freeman, *History of Europe*

Q On a trip to Mexico, my boyfriend and I went to a bullfight. It was horrible—a screaming crowd cheering the torture of a cornered, crazed animal. They should hang their heads in shame. After 20 minutes, we left. Why do people support these atrocities?

—E. L.

A Many tourists go out of a sense of curiosity and are shocked by what they see. But even if they walk out, as you did, the damage has been done, because the money they paid for admission has gone to the bullfight promoters, and that's all they care about. That's why the Mexican and Spanish people working to outlaw bullfighting in their countries ask us to please not even go in to bullfights.

Typically, a bull is worn to exhaustion by the time the picadors drive lances into his back and neck muscles, impairing his ability to lift his head. By the time the matador appears, the bull is even weaker from blood loss and is dizzy from being run in circles.

The horses used in bullfights also suffer. They are old and usually drugged. Wet newspaper is stuffed in their ears, and often their vocal cords are cut so the audience will not hear their cries. They wear long blankets to hide their entrails, which spill out when they are gored and disemboweled.

Mexico also holds baby bullfights. Baby bulls, some only a few weeks old, are stabbed to death by spectators, including many children. Then the tail and ears of the fully conscious calf are chopped off, and he is left to lie in his own blood.

Some U.S. states allow "bloodless bullfighting"—horrors wherein the terrified bulls are tormented and usually slaughtered immediately after they are taken from the ring.

Please tell your travel agent you are opposed to bullfighting and will not stay at any resort that has added a bullfight arena as part of its complex. Urge your friends to do the same. When we all protest and stay away from bullfights, they will die out. And I'm pretty sure anyone reading this book feels the same way I do—that this can't happen too soon.

THE GREYHOUND GIG

Q There is a greyhound-racing track in my city. There's also a group here that tries to find good homes for the retired racing dogs, so would you say this makes greyhound racing okay?

— T. R.

A Bravo to the people working to find homes for retired greyhounds. And a giant hiss to the greyhound racing industry for capitalizing on these good peoples' efforts by trying to make the public think this rights what's wrong with greyhound racing. It doesn't. It's a Band-Aid on a broken leg.

Only about 30 percent of greyhounds bred for the industry ever become racers. Then they spend their lives, except for races, in 3- x 3- x 4-foot crates. I'll never forget attending a swap meet near a greyhound track in Mesa, Ariz., and hearing the dogs crying from their crates in the

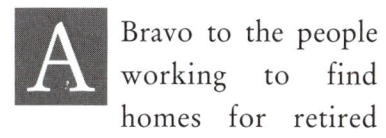

> *"Since adopting our first greyhound, Penny Smiles . . . and learning how special every greyhound is, we have become active in finding homes for as many of these wonderful dogs as possible. . . . We are outraged that we live in a society that continues to condone greyhound racing."*
>
> — S. N., From *Greyhound Network News*

105-degree heat. The 70 percent of greyhounds that never become racers are shot, euthanized, clubbed to death, or sold to laboratories.

It gets worse. Virtually every trainer believes dogs run faster if they're trained on living lures rather than mechanical ones, so the greyhounds pursue and mutilate rabbits, kittens, cats, chickens, puppies, small dogs, and other small creatures. Rabbits' legs are often broken so their cries will excite the dogs; guinea pigs are often used because they scream without "help" while dangling from a pole. The bloody, tattered animals are used over and over, as long as they have a scrap of life in them.

Greyhounds are such lovely, gentle dogs that trainers must "use" approximately five little animals to train each dog to go against his instincts. Often they cage a dog with a kitten or rabbit and starve him until he kills his cage companion.

Owners whose states prohibit the use of live lures ship their dogs for training to states such as Florida, Texas, and Kansas, where any laws against live lures are so watered down that they're ineffective. Such weak laws only serve as propaganda for the greyhound industry when it wants to open another track.

Let's help rid this country of its greyhound blight by boycotting greyhound races and asking our families and friends to do the same.

SKIP THIS RIDE

> *"It's simple. We do not have the right to use other creatures for pleasure or profit."*
> —Actress Kim Basinger, testifying before the House Committee on Agriculture in a hearing on animals in entertainment

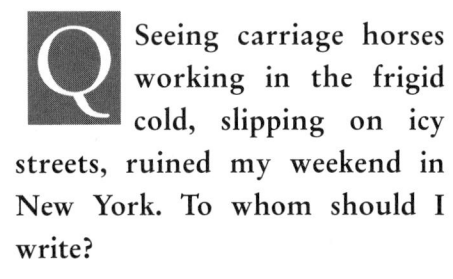

Q Seeing carriage horses working in the frigid cold, slipping on icy streets, ruined my weekend in New York. To whom should I write?

— Ginny R.

A Since you wrote to me, Jackie, a seven-year-old mare, was electrocuted in Manhattan when she stepped on a Con Edison Service box cover near Park Avenue. She was one of many horses who have died pulling carriages in New York City. Write to the Mayor of New York, City Hall, New York, NY 10007.

I urge people who see carriage horses in other cities to write to the mayors of those cities too. Scottsdale, Ariz., for example, has several carriage horses plodding through incredible heat all day. Philadelphia has many miserable carriage horses, suffering just like those in New York. I also think it's good to call out, "Shame on you," to carriage horse drivers and riders as they go by, to give them something to think about.

Public outcry has brought about carriage-horse bans in Palm Beach, Fla., Santa Fe, N.M., Las Vegas, Nev., London, Paris, and Toronto.

Rattlesnake Roundups

Q Are rattlesnake roundups real or is my Texan friend winding me up?

— Todd R.

A Unfortunately, they're real. These celebrations of cruelty are held primarily to boost shaky male egos, when what's really needed is extensive therapy.

> "The greatness of a nation and its moral progress can be judged by the way its animals are treated."
> — Mohandas K. Gandhi

Every spring, dozens of towns in the southern United States sponsor rattlesnake roundups. Months before, usually using sharp hooks, snake hunters collect the snakes during winter hibernation when they are weak. In some states, the hunters spray gasoline into the dens to drive out the snakes, but many die inside their dens. So do the rabbits, foxes, skunks, tortoises, burrowing owls, non-poisonous snakes, frogs, and many other animals that share dens with the rattlesnakes. Then the hunters store the snakes in boxes and sacks, without food or water, until the big day.

At the roundups, men (and a few women) loudly and proudly torture the weak, pitiful snakes, who feel pain, fear, heat, cold, hunger, and thirst just like other animals. The celebrants tease, kick, stomp on, and behead the snakes before cooking their insides and selling their skins.

Please help by never buying shoes, belts, or other items made from snakeskin, and by writing state and congressional lawmakers, asking them to outlaw rattlesnake roundups.

Also, avoid using the word "snake" to describe a lowlife human being. These poor animals need all the help they can get to shed the bad image humans have given them.

THE SHAME OF SPAIN

> *"Because animals lack a language we can understand, we listen only to our own thin excuses for treating them so abominably."*
>
> —Jon Wynne-Tyson, *The Extended Circle: A Dictionary of Humane Thought*

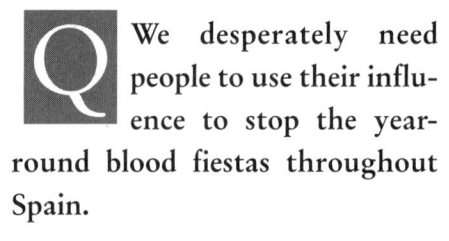

Q We desperately need people to use their influence to stop the year-round blood fiestas throughout Spain.

Here's a sampling:

* In Gijon, swimmers rip ducks apart.
* In Fuenlabrada, locals beat cows and bulls, wrench off their horns and sexually abuse them with spikes. After four hours of torture in 100-degree heat, the pitiful animals drink from pools of their own blood, and then locals stab them to death.
* In Bulgarra, locals break terrified young cows' legs and backs, then hack them to death.

* Many villages hang living chickens upside down, and men ride by on horseback and pull off the chickens' heads.
* In Manganeses de la Polverosa, a live goat dressed in women's underwear is thrown 50 feet from the church tower, then eaten.
* In Coria, hundreds of darts are blown at 14 bulls through blowpipes. Hits in the eyes or testicles are applauded. When the bulls collapse, they are blinded, castrated, and stabbed to death.

— Valentin C.

Everyone, please write to the Spanish ambassador. State your outrage, demand that the fiestas end, and emphasize that until they do, you and your friends will boycott all Spanish merchandise and travel.

His Excellency the Ambassador
The Spanish Embassy
24 Belgrave Square
London SW1 8QA, England

His Excellency the Ambassador
The Embassy of Spain
2375 Pennsylvania Ave., NW
Washington, DC 20037 USA
202-728-2340

Report all Spanish blood fiestas to:
Fight Against Animal Cruelty in Europe (FAACE)
20 Shakespeare St., Southport,
Merseyside PR8 5AB, U.K.

Chapter 8

Is This Cut Necessary?

Chester, one of the Silver Springs monkeys, watched longingly as Alex Pacheco, working undercover, left the lab each night. The case, detailed in the book Monkey Business, *caused Alex and Ingrid to launch the animal rights movement.*

Animal Research: Big Business

Q Isn't animal experimentation necessary for the well-being of humans?

— D.T.

A Yes, but only to the well-being of the experimenters who have to cut up given numbers of animals to get their grants renewed year after year and have no desire or impetus to switch to modern methods.

> "*The facts continue multiplying that refute the barbaric practice of animal experimentation in the name of human health and longevity. Yet the efforts by the medical establishment to justify this practice continue unabated.... The medical establishment threatens us with dire consequences if animal experimentation is stopped. This is a sham, a weapon being used to ensure continued funding*"
>
> — Murray J. Cohen, M.D., *Chicago Tribune*, Apr. 8, 1986

The vivisection industry has grown into a monster, a politically powerful conglomerate of institutions, experimenters, drug companies, animal supply companies, and medical supply companies, even corporations that produce miniature guillotines to behead rats and mice in laboratories. The fuel that keeps these companies going is animals. It's reached the point where they now shock, drug, slice, and dice more than *22 million* animals a year!

By now, we in the United States should all have eternal life, not to mention eternal youth.

Instead, people in 14 other industrialized countries in the world have longer life expectancies than people in the United States.

Med School Maneuvers

> "When I was a medical student, we went into the physiology and the pharmacology laboratories and did animal experiments, which we knew were worthless and the teachers knew were worthless, but we had to go through that ritual."
>
> — Robert S. Mendelsohn, M.D., Interviewed on CFRB, Toronto

Q The instructors at the medical school on my campus still make the students experiment on animals. What can a bunch of us students who hate this do about it?

— Melissa R

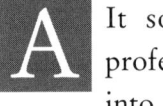

A It sounds like these professors need a jolt into modern medicine. In Britain, no animals have been used in medical schools for the last century, and more than half of the 126 medical schools in the U.S. now have eliminated practicing on animals.

They now use contemporary and more reliable teaching aids such as Harvey, a life-size cardiology simulator mannequin complete with carotid, brachial, radial, and femoral pulses, venous pulsations, pericardial movements, respiration, blood pressure, heart sounds, and other life-like features. Scientists have also perfected artificial skin and bone marrow and, from human brain cells, a "microbrain" with which to study tumors. We can now produce vaccines from cell cultures and test irritancy on egg membranes. These are just a few of many modern, more accurate replacements for animals.

To get the profs' attention, do what activists did at the University of North Carolina. On registration day, they quietly stationed themselves at the entrances to the med building and gave each incoming med student a cordial hello and a packet of information on the use of alternatives to animals in medical education. The activist students actually had med students lined up to receive the packets.

Is This Cut Necessary? 127

You can also stir things up by running PETA's film, "Dog Lab," shot undercover in a medical school, in a busy place like the cafeteria. The film is graphic, effective, and free from PETA. Good luck!

Testing Drugs

Q But shouldn't we test drugs on animals?
— Laura L.

A No. Animals have different reactions to drugs than people. For example, aspirin can be poisonous to cats and has no effect on fever in horses; benzene causes leukemia in humans but not in mice; insulin produces birth defects in animals, but not in humans; thalidomide produces birth defects in humans, but not in animals, and so on.

> *"Vivisection can only be defended by showing it to be right that one species should suffer in order that another species be happier.... If we cut up beasts simply because they cannot prevent us, and because we are backing our own side in the struggle for existence, it is only logical to cut up imbeciles, criminals, enemies, or capitalists for the same reason."*
> — C. S. Lewis, *The Problem of Pain*

Of the drugs the U.S. Food and Drug Administration approved between 1976 and 1985, more than 50 percent have since been removed from the market or relabeled because of serious side effects. So much evidence has accumulated about the differences in the effects chemicals have on animals and humans that government officials often do not act on findings from animal studies. Quantum pharmacology and in vitro tests give us far greater protection than tests on animals.

The Animal Welfare Act

> "If a being suffers, there can be no moral justification for refusing to take that suffering into consideration."
>
> — Peter Singer, *Animal Liberation*

Q Doesn't the Animal Welfare Act protect the animals from painful experiments?

— F. H.

A It gives them about as much protection as an umbrella in a rockslide. The Act doesn't even include rats, mice, or animals traditionally used for food. It is basically a housekeeping act; animals can be starved, shocked, driven insane, even burned with a blowtorch (done to dogs and pigs for burn experiments), as long as the laboratory is kept clean.

🐾 🐾 🐾

Behind The Locked Laboratory Doors

> "During my medical education at the University of Basel, I found vivisection horrible, barbarous, and above all unnecessary."
>
> — Carl G. Jung, *Collected Works*

Q If animal researchers are unashamed of the work they do and if they aren't cruel to animals, why don't they let the public in on their work?

— Dale G.

A What a good question! This is a social, not a medical, issue. Rather than treating it as an absolute that brooks no discussion, rather than shoring up security in their laboratories for fear someone will find out what the animals are going through, let the researchers take their cases to the public—open their laboratory doors, invite reporters and photograph hers inside, and let everyone know what this controversy is all about.

This may sound like a good idea, and it is, but you can bet your bottom dollar it will never happen, for one simple reason: The researchers wouldn't dare, because they would be run out of town. Imagine people's reaction when they saw such totally worthless experiments as: rotate kittens eyeballs, then make them jump from a high platform onto a plank in a pan of water (University of Oregon); shock squirrel monkeys in "fear conditioning" chambers (Stanford); shock rats' feet until the animals reached a pathetic state of learned helplessness, also scald their tails with hot water (University of North Carolina); harness cats fitted with "cranial implants" to treadmills and subject them to tail and paw shocks, producing "excessive struggling" and crying out (UCLA), and so on and on and on, to the tune of millions of animals a year, all to keep their funding coming.

A Not-So-Noble Nobel Laureate

Q I read in *Time* magazine that DNA discoverer and Nobel laureate James D. Watson put down the animal rights movement during a visit to a biology class at the Sidwell Friends School in Washington, D.C. I thought he was pretty awful to say, "The logical conclusion is we won't do any research and will spend all our resources making monkeys happy. I don't like monkeys."
Isn't it scary that people like him who are able to experiment on monkeys don't even like them?

"I would rather a butcher slaughter my dog than have him fall into the hands of research scientists."

— Julie Mayo, R.N.

— D. R.

A It's scary and this coldness appears to be a pre-requisite to becoming an animal researcher. Personally, I find it especially telling and chilling that researchers call the animals they experiment on "preparations."

Watson's remark reminded me of this moving account written by Ian Cook of Atlanta, which appeared in *Creative Loafing* magazine:

"For nine months during '89 and '90, I was employed as a primate technician at Yerkes Primate Research Center [one of seven U.S. primate research centers] . . . I have seen lit matches applied to the finger of an orangutan to make her release the bars of a cage . . . many chimps at Yerkes are short the usual number of digits and ears . . . some apes have holes in their skulls where monitoring equipment was once implanted. Some are ex-addicts who shake around in their concrete boxes all day . . . some of the apes were rejects from sign-language projects and signaled frantically as I passed."

Obviously, the researchers are not yet able to vivisect the feelings out of their "preparations."

SWALLOWING PEE — GULP!

> *"I used to take Premarin until PETA told me about the nightmare and suffering the horses go through for its manufacture. The slaughter of the mares' innocent babies is a crime against nature."*
>
> — Brigitte Bardot

Q My 15-year-old mare is my pride and joy. I care about all animals, but I want to do something specifically for horses. Is this selfish?

— Jill J.

A Hay, every little bit helps!

How about telling the world about Premarin's hidden ingredient: horse misery? Millions of women take this Wyeth-Ayerst drug to alleviate menopausal symptoms, but few know that they're swallowing estrogen synthesized from the urine from pregnant mares. To produce it, approximately 75,000 mares are impregnated, fitted with rubber urine-collection bags, and confined to small stalls for half a year. Wyeth-Ayerst encourages farmers to limit the mares' drinking water so their urine will have more concentrated estrogens. This results in the dehydrated mares struggling and sometimes injuring themselves during water-distribution times.

A few fillies replace the worn out mares on the pee lines, but most of the approximately 75,000 foals born each year go, along with the worn out mares, straight to the slaughterhouse.

In 1998, Robert Redford, Sylvester Stallone, and Richard Gere heard of the foals' fate from PETA and adopted four of them, who are now safe and sound.

I'm sending you PETA's free Premarin pack, which includes a list of the excellent, natural alternatives to Premarin. Help horses and people by sharing this information with your family, friends, and doctors and in letters to newspapers and magazines.

Chapter 9

Odds And Ends And Beginnings

When the PETA staff came together from around the world for a conference in June, 1999, they gathered outside the PETA headquarters building in Norfolk, Va., for this photo. Photo by Tal Ronnen

A Catholic Nun Speaks Out For The Animals

Q I am a Catholic nun who urges clergy of all faiths to speak out on behalf of animals. When God created the world, He created the animals before us. We humans were the last beings He put on this Earth. He designed the early world to be like heaven, with people and mammals and birds and fish and reptiles all living together in peace. We were to care for the animals, not persecute them. Because of the original sin, we are where we are—in a troubled world in which we destroy animals on a massive scale without a thought for their feelings or rights.

> "I swear that I think now that every living thing without exception has an eternal soul. I swear that I think there is nothing but immortality."
>
> — Walt Whitman

Catholic nun and animal advocate Sister Mary Vianney cuddles Muffin, who had been returned to the local animal shelter twice before Sister Mary adopted her and won her trust.

Each day, the cries of billions of animals, all marvelous creations of God, go unheard in animal factories and slaughterhouses. Let us address this agony. Many, myself included, find a vegetarian diet satisfying, healthful, and, best of all, kind.

I am appalled that we experiment on millions of animals every year. They suffer tremendously in our laboratories. Surely no good can come out of such cruelty to God's creatures.

I got my little dog Muffin at a nearby animal shelter. She had been returned there, rejected, twice. So I had to work with her until she came to trust me. It took a while, but now she's just as perky and self-confident as you please. Just like Muffin, each animal has a distinct personality. An animal feels pain as we do, and if we have dominion over animals surely we are to use this power to protect them. We need to extend our compassion to them. I believe that they will be in heaven with us, as they were originally.

If this seems mind-boggling, well, isn't all creation?

— Sister Mary Vianney

A Thank you so much, Sister Mary, for speaking out for the animals with such compassion and eloquence. I hope your message will be picked up and quoted far and wide.

No Souls? No Rights?

"If you went to the pearly gates and it said, 'No pets allowed,' most people would think twice about stepping inside."

— Rev. Gary Kowalski

Q My boyfriend Jeff says that because animals have no souls, they have no rights. What's your take on this?

— J. L.

A Isn't it funny how the most complicated questions have the simplest answers? In this case, to see that Jeff is wrong, all one has to do is look into an animal's eyes.

Even the word "animal," a PETA member pointed out to me, is derived from the Latin word "anima," which means soul.

The great humanitarian and Christian theologian Albert Schweitzer lamented the fact that Christianity excluded the animals from its teachings because it wanted a system of ethics that prescribed for humans their behavior toward other humans in clear, reasonable commandments without complicated demands.

"But ethics is avoiding a position that is already lost," he wrote. "Thought cannot avoid the ethic of reverence and love for all life. It will abandon the old confined system of ethics and be forced to recognize the ethics that knows no bounds."

Personally, I think it's quite possible that the first ones through the pearly gates will be walking on four legs.

CONVERT YOUR CLERGYPERSON INTO A CREATURE PREACHER

Q When I asked our pastor why he never spoke about the rights of animals, he copped out by saying that when he talks about love this includes the animals. How can I change his attitude?

— George A.

> *"As a Bishop of the Church of God, I am ashamed to say that the Church . . . has almost completely ignored the animal kingdom."*
>
> — Rt. Rev. John Chandler White

A Open his eyes and heart and make him a believer—in animal rights, that is—by contacting the area clergy association. Usually these groups meet once a month and are hungry for programs for these meetings. You (alone or with another animal advocate) can offer to give a program. Show "We Are All Noah," Professor Tom Regan's 30-minute video made especially for the clergy (available from the Culture and Animals Foundation, 3509 Eden Croft Dr., Raleigh, NC 27612). Following this persuasive film, pass out literature and answer questions about animal rights.

If you can't track down a monthly meeting, make an appointment with your clergyperson for a private presentation.

Also, earlier in this chapter is a beautiful letter from a Catholic nun. Show this to your minister too.

Blessings!

Ending Dissection: One Student's Story

> *"Next time you have an opportunity to intercede in behalf of a tiny being, let your natural compassion overpower your embarrassment and be proud to explain that no life is too small to deserve consideration."*
>
> — Sherry Hamilton Ziemski

Q Thanks for the ton of free dissection information, including the wonderful "Classroom Cut-Ups" video. With this material, I bravely fought against dissection in our school. I showed the video to the entire staff, including the principal. They agreed with me and now are on the animals' side and mine. Next, I gave presentations to each 7th through 10th grade science class, as well as to my science teacher.

When they all learned the awful truth, about 90 percent of them vowed to give up dissection, including my stubborn science teacher! Now that he knows the real story, he says dissection will never again take place in his teachings. He also has requested that I get a copy of "Classroom Cut-Ups" for him to show in class year after year, reaching hundreds of students.

All you need is love.

— Chani G.

A Chani, we love you. Bravo!

Anyone who wants a copy of "Classroom Cut-Ups," PETA's undercover video of dissection supply houses, can get it free from PETA.

EMERGENCY PROCEDURE

Q A fireman gave me this tip: If emergency personnel come to your door to evacuate you, don't argue or say, "Just let me get my dog, cat, etc." Instead, say, "Thanks. I'll get my baby." They then will go right on to the next house, leaving you free to get your companions out.

> "I have a dream. I see humankind understanding that the spirit which sings in our hearts sings as well in the hearts of the other animals."
> — John Robbins, *Diet for a New America*

— Phyllis B.

A Thanks. And of course our leashes, cat carrier, etc., are always handy, so we then can make like a banana and split. If you have horses or other large animals, now's a good time to arrange for their safekeeping in case of floods or fires.

The Chain Of Violence

> "The most dangerous thing that can happen to a child is for the child to torture or kill an animal and get away with it."
>
> — Margaret Mead

Q I read in the paper that when a friendly cat meandered into a McNary, Ore., high school football player's home, he and another student clubbed the cat to death.

Football coach Tom Smythe outraged me with his comments: "He didn't rape, maim, or pillage anyone. He committed a foolish act that cost a dumb animal its life. So, let's not drag this out forever."

Do you think such an attitude affects the students one way or the other?

— C.M.

A Definitely. As a person of authority, this coach's cavalier attitude could contribute to his students' further delinquency. It probably already has. Less than a year earlier, seven McNary students, including four football players, were charged with beating an opossum and setting him on fire. They videotaped the animal's agony, then showed the tape in a class when the teacher was away.

Studies have shown that a high percentage of prison inmates charged with violent crimes had early records of animal abuse that should have been dealt with seriously. They often started with the family dog or cat. Some learned to abuse animals from their parents. Serial killer Ted Bundy, linked to 50 murders, claimed he spent much of his childhood torturing animals with his grandfather. Albert DeSalvo, the "Boston Strangler," who killed 13 women, as a kid put cats and dogs in orange crates, then shot arrows through the crates.

I doubt if Coach Smythe would take lightly a violent act against a member of his own family; yet attitudes like his foster such acts. PETA urged that this coach undergo remedial training and that the cat-killers be prosecuted and sentenced to the full extent of the law.

Gruesome Greetings

Q Some of those cute puppies, kittens, ducklings, and other animals on greeting cards, calendars and posters seem posed unrealistically. What am I really looking at?

— Jill S.

> *"Having the right heroes will take you right through the trouble spots in your life."*
>
> — Warren Buffet

A That "S" must be for Sherlock. Yes, many of these sweet creatures have been to the taxidermist. Next time you spot such a photo, let the shop owner and, if possible, the publisher know exactly how you feel about this cruelty and deception.

Signs Of The Times

Q I put my favorite animal rights posters on my car when and where I want them. First, I laminate the poster. Then I glue it to a piece of magnetic sign material that flops onto the side of my car. My interchangeable items allow for great diversity and for removal at night so my vehicle won't be defaced. Bon voyage!

> *"No army can withstand the strength of an idea whose time has come."*
>
> — Victor Hugo

— **Gary D.**

A Thanks for a super tip, Gary.

Life In The (Unbearably) Slow Lane

> "To know oneself, one should assert oneself."
> — Albert Camus

Q My friend wants an aquarium for his birthday. What do you think of this idea?
— Marie H.

A Not much, unless you know some fish criminals to put in it. So many aquariums are like stark prison cells, and the worst are the glass bowls with just one or two goldfish and nothing to enhance their barren habitat. These little prisons give new meaning to the phrase, "bored, lonely, and a long way from home."

Christine Jackson watched a leopard shark swim back and forth in front of the cement "coral" in a local store's aquarium. She said, "He was like a leopard pacing endlessly in his cage, with no hope of escape."

Homebound Activism

> "Never doubt that a small group of thoughtful committed citizens can change the world; indeed, it's the only thing that ever has."
> — Margaret Mead

Q I'd love to be on the front lines of animal rights, but I'm raising a three-year-old daughter and caring for my dad, who's in a wheelchair. My husband loves animals, too, but he works 12 hours a day to keep a roof over our heads. What can we do?
— E. K.

A For people busier than a wallpaper hanger with a broken arm and the seven-year-itch, the direct action of choice is postcards.

Get a sizable stack of postcards and stamps, or pre-stamped postcards. Keep them and the addresses of the major stations near the TV and radio. When a show or commercial promotes or trivializes animal abuse, jot down the station, program, name, scene, and date.

When a viewer cares enough to write, producers take notice. This is a great way to make a difference for the animals. Plus, mail clerks and clerical workers along the way often will read and think about your message.

🐾 🐾 🐾

YEASTS AND ALBERT SCHWEITZER

Q How do animal rightists feel about the killing of 150 million or so yeasts every time a loaf of bread is baked?

— Get Real

"The only true happiness comes from squandering ourselves for a purpose."

— William Cowper

A Some day the yeasts may rise. For now, we have all we can do to help fellow Earthlings we know or strongly suspect to be sentient.

Albert Schweitzer warned of the problems and responsibilities that a boundless ethic brings with it. He said each of us "must live daily from judgment to judgment, deciding each case as it arises, as wisely and mercifully as we can."

Escaping Blizzardsville

> "A friend is a gift you give yourself."
> —Robert Louis Stevenson

Q I'm the only animal rights activist I know. How do I keep from feeling like I'm shoveling snow in a blizzard?

— Lew L.

A Brighten your life and lighten your load—link up with others. Post notices in markets, bookstores, newspapers, on the Web and other places saying, "Join new animal rights group. Call Lew at 123-4567."

Ask local radio announcers to broadcast your message. At a fair or other busy place, man a table with a sign-up sheet for interested people.

I'm sending you PETA's "Starting a Group" folder, free to everyone who writes for it. Remember, a group can start with two people.

Good luck!

Flesh And Blood "Things"?

> All truth passes through three stages. First, it is ridiculed. Second, it is violently opposed. Third, it is accepted.
> — Arthur Schopenhauer

Q An "it" is a thing. Animals are flesh and blood, so why are they called "it" and "things"?

— Joel T.

A This cold custom is fallout from Western civilization's failure to consider animals worthy in their own right. It's one step lower than the subordinate status our language accorded women for centuries, until the women's movement demanded that the universal "man" be changed to "person" or "individual."

Animal users and abusers depersonalize them even further than "it" to better exploit them. Hunters call them "game." Experimenters call them "preparations" or "models." Meat producers call them "stock" or "livestock."

As Arthur Schopenhauer said in *On the Basis of Morality*, ". . . because Christian morality leaves animals out of account . . . they are mere 'things', mere means to any ends whatsoever. They can therefore be used for vivisection, hunting, coursing, bullfights, and horse racing, and can be whipped to death as they struggle along with heavy carts of stone."

But the time has come for all speciesist terms to topple into oblivion. Today, most people realize that every dog or cat in their lives has a unique personality. So does every other animal, including, I've learned firsthand, each chicken, cow, turkey, and pig. A former curator of a large aquarium said, "Every fish has a distinct personality and, furthermore, I'm sure every bumblebee does, too."

That they do is no more amazing than the other wonders that surround us.

Today, ground-breaking new books are flying in the face of the animal exploiters' self-serving taboo against "anthropomorphizing" animals. Books like *Animal Minds* by Donald R. Griffin, *The Human Nature of Birds* by Theodore X. Barber, and *When Elephants Weep*, by Jeffrey Moussaieff Mason and Susan McCarthy, are detailing revolutionary examples of individual animals' strivings, feelings, intelligence, and experiences.

I call animals "he" or "she." If I don't know an animal's sex, I randomly choose either of these pronouns. Often a newspaper editor has changed my "he" or "she" to an "it," and once I dropped my weekly newspaper column, because a new editor refused to change them back.

"What about an insect?", you might ask. Well, I still sometimes slip and say "it." But not around bees!

Justice Prevails

> *"Through you and decent people like you, poor creatures like Sheba do have a voice."*
>
> — Judge Norman A. Barron in response to activist Norma M.

Q To encourage other judges to act courageously against animal abusers, would you please print the enclosed "Comments at Sentencing" of Judge Norman A. Barron in the case of the State v. Jose I. Canales in the Superior Court of the State of Delaware, July 9, 1993?

— Trudy K.

A With pleasure, Trudy. Here they are, in near-entirety. I especially like his last paragraph.

"The late pacifist, Mahatma Gandhi, once said that `[T]he greatness of a nation . . . can be judged by the way its animals are treated.' If the letters and petitions this court has received in response to this case is any indication, then I can say with assurance that our national greatness is secure.

From Green Cove Springs, Florida, to . . . Houston, Texas, Americans have expressed their outrage over your despicable crime.

"Hitler's Gestapo could not conjure up a method of torture more apt to instill in its victim such a sense of utter terror, nor one which would produce such agonizing pain. The fact that Sheba was just a dog makes this crime no less reprehensible. As Jeremy Bentham, the great English jurist and philosopher, once observed, 'The question is not, can they reason? Nor, can they talk? But can they suffer?' And at your hands Sheba Grayston suffered mightily. Listen to the words of her owner, Holly Grayston:

"'Sheba was a loving, gentle, well-trained beautiful dog that was not only my protector and companion, but she was my best friend for 11 years . . . I haven't been able to fall asleep at night since November. I had to be taken to the hospital and I don't even remember how I got there, but my mother thought I was having a nervous breakdown.

"'Sheba was operated on for 6 hours, screamed in pain through the night, had 3 cardiac arrests and died, and this was after she was beaten, raped, cut up inside, and thrown in the weeds to die. But she didn't die right away, she suffered massive pain for 2 days.

"'I don't think I'll ever be able to get over this. I can't talk or think about her without crying. Jose Canales is an evil man that the seldom times I can sleep gives me nightmares. I never really bothered this man, and he killed my dog and broke my heart.'

"The veterinary surgeon, Dr. Jill Sammarco, who operated on Sheba in her final hours of life on November 15, 1992, had this to say about your unspeakable crime:

"... 'I have no doubt that Sheba died as a direct result of systemic infection caused by the infliction of a wound which penetrated deeply into the abdominal cavity .... The object used to inflict these injuries had a sharp edge since tissues were cut rather than torn ... the object must have been driven with some force to a depth of at least 10 inches into the dog's vagina ... I have never been so horrified by the injuries caused to an animal by a human being ...'

"... I believe beyond a doubt that you unleashed Sheba and lured her into your apartment where you proceeded to brutalize this helpless and defenseless 12-year-old animal...

"... In imposing sentence, I am fully aware of my ethical obligations under the code of judicial conduct. I recognize that under Canon 3 of that code, I should be unswayed by partisan interests, public clamor, or fear of criticism. Had there not been the public outcry evidenced in this case, my sentence would be the same. I have never had the good fortune of having a pet dog, either when I was a child or now as an adult. In a real sense, I have missed out on a unique relationship where, in the words of the late Sen. George Vest of Missouri, a faithful family dog `guards the sleep of his pauper master as if he were a prince.'

"The maximum sentence permitted by law is totally appropriate in this case. I have presided over many criminal trials involving infamous defendants who committed gruesome murders and unprovoked rapes. But never have I felt the utter revulsion which your actions have inspired.

The bestiality of your conduct will not be condoned by your insobriety at the time of the incident, because intoxication is not a defense. This senseless, barbaric crime of utter perversion ranks as one of the vilest, most horrific acts of cruelty ever presented before this court.

"Leonardo da Vinci once predicted that '[T]he time will come when men such as I will look upon the murder of animals as they now look upon the murder of human beings.' Da Vinci's prediction is one which you, Jose Canales, might well reflect upon as the days ahead turn into weeks, the weeks turn into months and the months into years."

Seeing's Believing

> *Because I am a civil rights activist, I am also an animal rights activist. Animals and humans suffer and die alike. Violence causes the same pain, the same spilling of blood, the same stench of death, the same arrogant, cruel, and vicious taking of life. We shouldn't be part of it."*
>
> *— Dick Gregory*

Q Eddie, my boyfriend, refuses to quit eating meat or to believe that animal suffering is a as widespread as PETA says it is. He says PETA is no authority on animals, that it's just a propaganda mill that pulls off outrageous stunts to get publicity for itself. What can I tell him?

— Kelly B.

A Tell Eddie to take off the blinders while you show him the "The Diner," available from PETA, and other videos listed in the appendix of this book under "Videos and Audio tapes." Pictures really can be worth a thousand words.

PETA is an authority, in spades, on animal suffering. One of our toughest jobs is choosing which horrors we will focus on on any given day—there are so many vying for our attention. Any decent person who saw the cruelty we here at PETA deal with on a daily basis would join our sometimes outlandish stunts to make the public face the facts. It's tough to break through the walls society has put up of not wanting to know, and the animal abuse industries thrive on this apathy. But the animals, billions of them, desperately need everyone to know—and care.

I doubt that Eddie will remain unmoved, but if he does, it's time for you to move—away from him and toward a guy with a heart in his chest and a brain in his head instead of rocks in both places.

Awareness Shines Forth From All Creatures

Q Where do creatures low on the evolutionary scale fit into animal rights? Don't we have to draw the line somewhere?

— John G.

> *"It is just like man's vanity and impertinence to call an animal dumb because it is dumb to his dull perceptions."*
>
> — Mark Twain, *What is Man?*

A It's getting harder and harder to show favoritism as we learn that awareness is downright rampant among Earthlings.

For instance, octopuses, ranked with slugs, snails, and clams as mollusks, are bright and curious. In rooms with several aquariums, they sometimes crawl out of their own tank and into another where they see something that interests them.

When one of two balls had a fish behind it and the other a mild electric shock, octopuses soon learned to choose the right ball. But other octopuses that watched them learned even faster. The latter, after seeing the trained animals perform four times, immediately and invariably chose the right ball, even five days later.

However, octopuses are very intelligent and don't need negative reinforcement like shocking. For example, an octopus can quickly figure out how to unscrew a jar lid, and an octopus that observes her can unscrew it even faster.

In the sea, where they belong, these willowy, winsome creatures form relationships with other octopuses and communicate through color change, skin texture, and other ways of which we are unaware. In the blink of an eye, they can change their skin color from pale white to deep maroon and skin texture from lumpy to smooth. They have superb eyesight. They are curious and like to adorn their homes with ocean trinkets ("an octopus's garden"). If they can get their hard beak through an opening, they can get their whole body through it. They are gentle and shy. They never attack people; they run from them, exhaling jet-like bursts of water through sacks that propel them swiftly away.

I knew a relative of the octopus, a snail. She was in an aquarium of my father's. She used to crawl out of the tank at night and travel around the kitchen counter it was set upon. Sometimes she laid eggs there. Then she crawled back into the aquarium and remained there during the day.

Octavia, however, couldn't climb out. The 58-pound octopus was caught and sealed in a cramped 4- x 5-foot tank at San Pedros's Cabrillo Marine Aquarium. Attendance tripled. Weeks later, Octavia pulled out a plastic pipe, the water drained from her tank, and she died.

Don't you think that examples like these make a good case for leaving all sea creatures in the seas and not confining them in aquariums?

Don't you agree that the more we learn about each creature, the more impossible it becomes to decide who is the more worthy?

APPENDIX

BOOKS

GENERAL ANIMAL AND ANIMAL RIGHTS:

Animal Liberation, by Peter Singer. The profound social and moral appeal to conscience, decency, and justice that inspired the animal rights movement, essential reading for supporter and skeptic alike. Available from PETA.

You Can Save the Animals, by Ingrid Newkirk. Vision, wisdom, and answers from PETA's president and co-founder, as she shares her personal feelings and experiences with animals and gives you hundreds of easy ways to help them in your everyday living. Available from PETA.

Fettered Kingdoms, by John Bryant. A moving, personal indictment of society's treatment of animals by a former Vice Chairman of the RSPCA.

Free the Animals, by Ingrid Newkirk. An animal liberator's riveting, true account of how she and other liberators pulled off daring animal rescues from laboratories, fur farms, and meat factories. Available from PETA.

The Extended Circle, A Dictionary of Humane Thought, edited by Jon Wynne-Tyson. A magnificent, inspiring anthology of thoughts regarding compassion for animals from famous people throughout history and in the present. Printed in U.K. by Villiers Publications Ltd., London N6.

Monkey Business, by Kathy Snow Guillermo. The inspiring true story of Alex Pacheco and Ingrid Newkirk; how they met, founded PETA, and took on the case of the Silver Spring monkeys that launched the animal rights movement. Available from PETA.

The American Hunting Myth, by Ron Baker. Hard facts about the state and federal "wildlife" agencies that perpetuate the "sport" of hunting.

What's Wrong With Hunting, compiled by the Fund for Animals. An entertaining and educational look at the practice of sport hunting in America, with accounts from Hollywood and sport celebrities. Available from the Fund for Animals.

Slaughterhouse, by Gail Eisnitz. A shocking look inside the U.S. meat industry.

Beyond the Bars: The Zoo Dilemma, by Virginia McKenna, Will Travers and Jonathan Wray

The Rose-Tinted Menagerie, by William Johnson. The cruelty and deprivation of animals in circuses and dolphinaria is exposed in shocking detail.

250 Things You Can Do to Make Your Cat Adore You, by Ingrid Newkirk. Fresh ideas, cat body language, holistic remedies, and real insight into a cat's point of view.

Stolen for Profit, by Judith Reitman. Exposes the pet theft trade.

Understanding Your Dog, by Michael Fox, D.V.M.

Old McDonald's Factory Farm, by David Coates. A chilling look inside the meat industry's animal factories.

Naked Empress, by Hans Ruesch. Exposes chemical and pharmaceutical industry corruption and vivisection as a racket that has become an endless source of profits and new diseases. Available from The Nature of Wellness (818-790-6384)

Slaughter of the Innocent, by Hans Reusch. Exposes the vivisection industry. Available from The Nature of Wellness (818-790-6384)

When Elephants Weep: The Emotional Lives of Animals, by Masson and McCarthy.

The Dreaded Comparison, Human and Animal Slavery, by Marjorie Spiegel. A powerful book with unforgettable photos; it can be read in an hour.

ANIMAL RIGHTS BOOKLETS

    The PETA Guide to Action for Animals. $2.00 from PETA
    The PETA Guide to Animal Liberation. $2.00 from PETA
    The PETA Guide to Compassionate Living. $2.00 from PETA
    2000 Shopping Guide for Caring consumers. $7.95 from PETA

VEGAN COOKBOOKS

The Compassionate Cook, by Ingrid Newkirk. Favorite vegan recipes from PETA staff and members. Available from PETA.

The New Farm Vegetarian Cookbook, The Book Publishing Company, P. O. Box 99, Summertown TN 38483-0180.

Instead of Chicken, Instead of Turkey, by Karen Davis. Vegan alternatives to poultry and eggs. Available from PETA and United Poultry Concerns.

Cooking with PETA. More than two hundred recipes, plus information on how and why to become vegetarian. Available from PETA.

HEALTH

Eat Right, Live Longer: Using the Natural Power of Foods to Age-Proof Your Body, by Neal Barnard, M.D. Available from PCRM and PETA.

Food for Life, by Neal Barnard, M.D., Available from PCRM and Crown Tree Paperbacks.

A Physician's Slimming Guide by Neal Barnard, M.D. Available from PETA and PCRM.

The McDougall Plan for Super Health, by John McDougall, M.D., and Mary McDougall.

Vegan Nutrition Pure and Simple, by Michael Klaper.

Diet for A New America, by John Robbins. Stillpoint Publishing. (Also has a wealth of animal rights and environmental information.)

May All Be Fed: Diet for a New World, by John Robbins, Avon Books.

Foods that Fight Pain, by Neal Barnard, M.D. Available from PCRM.

MAGAZINES

The Animals' Agenda (P.O. Box 25881, Baltimore, MD 21224)
A "must" for animal activists and everyone wanting to keep informed about the animal rights movement.
410-675-4566
Fax: 410-675-0066
Web site: www/animalsagenda.org
e-mail: office@animalsagenda.org

Vegetarian Times (4 High Ridge Rd., Stamford, CT 06905; 800-829-3340).

Newspaper

No Compromise, The Militant Direct Action Newspaper of Grassroots Animal Liberationists and Their Supporters
(P.O. Box 5236, Old Bridge, NJ 08857)
Web site: www.nocompromise.org
e-mail: NoComp@waste.org

Catalog

The Mail Order Catalog (free)
P.O. Box 180
Summertown, TN 38483
931-964-2241
800-695-2241
Fax: 931-964-2291
Web site: www.healthy-eating.com
catalog@usit.net

Large variety of vegetarian meat substitutes and other vegetarian foods, vegetarian cookbooks, and health, animal, and Native American books. Free catalog.

Video and Audio Tapes

Live Longer, Live Better, by Neal Barnard, M.D. 90 minutes. $9.95. Available from PCRM or PETA. Easy but powerful approach to permanent slimness, lowering cholesterol, and controlling your blood pressure, with interviews with leading experts, including one with Dean Ornish, M.D., on reversing heart disease.

Dairy Farm Investigation. 7 minutes. Available on loan from PETA.

Diet for a New America. PBS documentary. 60- and 30-minute versions. $19.95 from EarthSave International or PETA, or on loan from PETA.

The Diner. Responsible for getting many people to "go vegetarian" on the spot. 11 minutes. Available on loan from PETA.

Raw Footage, Raw Pain. Secret footage from inside an egg factory farm. 12 minutes. Available on loan from PETA.

The Down Side of Livestock Marketing. The abuse downed animals endure at stockyards and auctions. 18 minutes. Available from Farm Sanctuary.

Hidden Suffering. Inhumane conditions domestic fowl endure. 27 minutes. Available from Farm Animal Welfare Network.

Humane Slaughter? Shows poultry slaughter; concludes with plea to viewer to demand that poultry be included in Humane Slaughter Act and to become a vegetarian. Available from Farm Sanctuary.

The Pig Picture. The life of a factory-farmed pig. 17 minutes. Available from The Humane Farming Association.

Cheap Tricks. Traveling animal acts, narrated by Alec Baldwin. 12 minutes. $15.00. Available from PETA.

Zoochotic Report: A ZooCheck Investigation. Signs of madness and boredom in captive animals. Available from the Born Free Foundation.

The Ugliest Show on Earth. An undercover investigation of British circuses. 26 minutes. Available from Animal Defenders.

Dying to Please. "Swim with dolphins" programs and other marine mammal issues. Narrated by Michael Landon. Available from Focus on Animals.

The Other Barred. Sensitive documentary explores animals feelings by showing them in their cages without dialogue or commentary. 10 minutes. Suitable for all ages. Available from Bullfrog Films, Inc.

We Are All Noah. Prof. Tom Regan's film dedicated to the religious community, asking that we widen our circle of compassion. Available from:

Focus on Animals.
Bullfrog Films, Inc.
900-543-FROG
P.O. Box 149
Oley, PA 19547
Web site:
www.bullfrogfilms.com

Pyramid Flim & Video
310-828-7577
2801 Colorado Avenue
Santa Monica, CA 90404

Pro-Animal Groups

Action for Animals
P.O. Box 20184
Oakland CA 94620
510-652-5603

Animal Legal Defense Fund
127 4th St.
Petaluma CA 94952
707-769-7771
Fax: 707-769-0785
Web site: www.aldf.org
e-mail: info@aldof.org

Animal Liberation League
P.O. Box 7245
Minneapolis MN 55407

Animal Rights Foundation of Florida (ARFF)
P.O. Box 841154
Pembroke Pines, FL 33084
954-927-ARFF (2733)

Animal Rights Hawaii
P.O. Box 10845
Honolulu HI 96816-0845
808-941-9476

Animal Welfare Institute
P.O. Box 3650 or P.O. Box 3719
Georgetown Station
Washington, DC 20007
202-337-2332
Web site: www.animalwelfare.com
e-mail: awi@animalwelfare.com

Association of Veterinarians for Animal Rights (AVAR)
P.O. Box 208
Davis CA 95617-0208
530-759-8106

Beauty Without Cruelty
175 W. 12th St., 16C
New York NY 10011
212-989-8073

The Black Vegetarian Society
P.O. Box 14803
Atlanta GA 30324-1803
770-621-5056

Coalition to End Primate Experimentation (CEPE)
Organizers of the Primate Freedom Tour
P.O. Box 34293
Washington, DC 20043
888-391-8948
Web site: www.enviroweb.org\cepe
e-mail: CEPEmail@yahoo.com

Dissection Hotline
1-8000922-FROG (3764)

Doris Day Animal League
227 Massachusetts Ave. NE, Suite 100
Washingtopn DC 20002
202-546-1761
e-mail: ddal@aol.com
Provides information on federal legislation re. animals

Earth Island Institute
300 Broadway, Suite 28
San Francisco CA 94133
415-788-3666
Fax: 415-788-7324
e-mail: earthisland@earthisland.org
Supports projects for the preservation/restoration of the global environment

EarthSave
600 Distillery Commons, Suite 200
Louisville KY 40206
502-5890-7676
Web site: www.earthsave.org
e-mail: earthsave@aol.com
Provides environmental and health education, and materials and support for people becoming vegetarians

Elephant Alliance
6265 Cardeno Dr.
La Jolla CA 92037
619-454-4959

Pro-Animal Groups

Farm Sanctuary
3100 Aikens Rd.
Watkins Glen NY 14891
530-865-4622
Fax: 530-865-4622
Web site: www.farmsanctuary.org
Works to prevent abuses in animal farming through legislation, investigations, education and direct rescue programs. Operates shelters for rescued farm animals.

The Farm
Summertown, TN 38483
931-964-3574
Web site: www.thefarm.org
A vegetarian community with different branches, including an ecovillage training center, a book publishing company, a conference center, a video production center, and an extensive free mail order catalog (see "Catalogs," p. 152).

Focus on Animals
534 Red Bud Road
Winchester, VA 22603
540-665-2827

Friends of Animals
777 Post Rd., Suite 205
Darien CT 06820
203-656-1522

The Fund for Animals
8121 Georgia Ave., Suite 301
Silver Spring MD 20910
301-585-2591
Web site: www.fund.org
e-mail: fund4animals@fund.org

Greyhound Network News
P.O. Box 44272
Phoenix AZ 85064-4272

Hinduism Today
107 Kaholalele Road
Kapaa HI 96746-9304
Web site: www.hindu.org/ht

Humane Farming Association
1550 California St., Suite 6
San Francisco CA 94109
415-771-2253
Leads a national campaign to stop factory farms from misusing chemicals, abusing animals and misleading the public.

Humane Society of the United States (HSUS)
2100 L St., NW
Washington, DC 20037
202-452-1100
Web site: www.hsus.org

In Defense of Animals
131 Camino Alto, Suite E
Mill Valley, CA 94941
415-388-9641
Fax: 415-388-0388
Web site: www.idausa.org
e-mail: ida@idausa.org

Jewish Vegetarians of North America
6938 Reliance Road
Federalsburg, MD 20632
410-754-5550
e-mail: imossman@skipjack.bluecrab.org

Jews for Animal Rights
255 Humphrey St.
Marblehead, MA 01945
Web site:
host.envirolink.ofg/jar/jews_ar

Last Chance for Animals
8033 Sunset Blvd., Suite 35
Los Angeles, CA 90046
310-271-6096 or 888-88-ANIMAL
Fax: 310-271-1890
Web site: www.lcanimal.org
e-mail: info@lcanimal.org

Medical Research Modernization Committee
20145 Van Aken Blvd., #24
Shaker Heights, OH 44122
216-283-6702
Web site: www.mrmcmed.org
e-mail: mrmcmed@aol.com

Northwest Animal Rights Network (NARN)
1704 E. Galer
Seattle WA 98112
206-323-7301
Web site: www.narn.org

Pasado's Safe Haven
P.O. Box 171
Sultan WA 98294
360-793-9393
Web site: www.pasadosafehaven.org

People for the Ethical Treatment of Animals (PETA)
501 Front St.
Norfolk, VA 23510
757-622-PETA (7382)
Web site: www.peta-online.org
e-mail: peta@norfolk.infi.net

Performing Animal Welfare Society (PAWS)
P.O. Box 849
Galt, CA 95632
209-745-2606

Progressive Animal Welfare Society (PAWS)
15305 44th Avenue West
P.O. Box 1037
Lynnwood, WA 98046
425-787-2500
Web site: www.paws.org

Physicians Committee for Responsible Medicine (PCRM)
P.O. Box 6322
Washington, DC 20015
202-686-2210
Fax: 202-686-2216
Web site: www.pcrm.org
e-mail: pcrm@pcrm.org
Comprised of physicians and lay members; promotes nutrition, preventive medicine and ethical research; publishers of Good Medicine magazine.

Psychologists for the Ethical Treatment of Animals (PsyETA)
P.O. Box 1297
Washington Grove, MD 20800-1297
301-963-4751

Sea Shepherd Society
P.O. Box 628
Venice, CA 90294
310-301-SEAL (7325)
Fax: 310-574-3161
Web site: www.seashepherd.org

Society for Animal Protective Legislation
P.O. Box 3719
Georgetown Station
Washington, DC 20007
202-337-2334
A resource organization that tracks anti-fur and factory farming legislation

SPAY USA
1-800-248-SPAY (7729)
Helps people find low-cost veterinarians

United Animal Nations
5892 South Land Park Dr.
P.O. Box 188890
Sacramento, CA 95818
916-429-2457
Fax: 916-429-2456
Web site: wee.uan.org
e-mail: info@uan.org
Rescues animals from disasters in the U.S.

United Poultry Concerns (UPC)
12325 Seaside Rd.
Machipongo, VA 23405
757-678-7875

Vegan Action
P.O. Box 4353
Berkeley, CA 94704-0353
510-548-7377
Web site: www.vegan.org

Pro-Animal Groups 157

Vegan Outreach
211 Indian Dr.
Pittsburgh, PA 15238
Web site: www.veganoutreach.org
Distributes the informative booklet,
Why Vegan?

Wildlife 2000
4905 W. Lakeridge Rd.
Denver, Co. 80219
303-935-4495

Vegetarian Resource Group
P.O. Box 1463
Baltimore, MD 21203
410-366-8343
Fax: 410-366-8804
Web site: www.vrg.org

World Society for the Protection of Animals (WSPA)
P.O. Box 190
Boston, MA 02130
617-522-7000
Helps captive animals abroad and animals victimized by war and natural disasters worldwide.

CANADA

Calgary Animal Rights Coalition
41 6A St. NE
Calgary Alberta T2E 4A2
403-262-3458

ZooCheck Canada
3266 Yonge St., Ste. 1729
Toronto, Ontario M4N 3P6
416-285-1744

ENGLAND

Animal Aid
The Old Chapel
Bradford St.
Tonbridge
Kent TN9 1AW
44-1732-364546
Fax: 44-1732-366533
Web site: www.animalaid.org.uk

Born Free Foundation
3 Grove House
Foundry Lane
Norsham
West Sussex RH 13 5 PL
44-1403-240170
Fax: 44-1403-327838

British Union for the Abolition of Vivisection (BUAV)
16A Crane Grove
London N7 8NN
44-171-700-4888
Fax: 44-171-700-0252

Compassion in World Farming (CIWF)
Charles House
5A Charles St.
Petersfield
Hampshire GU32 3EH
44-1730-264208
Fax: 44-1730-260791

European Coalition to End Animal Experiments
16A Crane Grove
London N7 8NN
44-171-700-0252
e-mail: sariv@compuserve.com

League Against Cruel Sports
Sparling House
83-87 Union St.
London SE1 1SG
44-171-403-6155
Fax: 44-171-403-4532

Muslim Vegan/Vegetarian Society
59 Brey Towers
136 Adelaide Rd.
London NW3 3JU

Royal Society for the Protection of Animals (RSPCA)
The Manor House
The Causeway
Horsham
West Sussex RH12 1HG
44-1403-264181
Fax: 44-1403-241042

158 Living in Harmony with Animals

Vegan Society
Donald Watson House
7 Battle Road
St. Leonards-on-Sea
East Sussex TN37-7AA
44-1424-427393
Fax: 44-1424-717064

ADDITIONAL WEB SITES

The Animal Rights Resource Site
arrs.envirolink.org
One of the largest clearinghouses for animal rights information online

Coalition to Abolish the Fur Trade
www.banfur.com

Compassion Over Killing
www.cok-online.org
Has links to web sites focusing on campaigns against Macy's and Neiman Marcus fur sales. A good example of a local activist group with a focused online presence.

The Essene Cooperative's Homepage
www.inetex.com/joanne/

Factory Farming.com: The Truth Hurts
www.factory farming.com

HandiLinks to Vegetarian Organizations
www.ahandyguide.com/cat1/v/v26

Jesus Was a Vegetarian
www.Jesus-online.com

The Mining Co. Guide to Animal Rights
www.animalrights.miningco.com
Links to the latest alerts from animal rights organizations

National Institutes of Health-Current Animal Experiments Information
www-commons.cit.nih.gov\crisp\
(Scroll to "current award info" at bottom and fill in name of institution you are seeking information about)

Veg Source Interactive
www.vegsource.org
Many links to vegetarian information and discussion boards

Veg Web
www.vegweb.com
Hundreds of vegetarian recipes

The Veggies Animal Contact Directory
www.interalpha.net/customer/ecoslobs/veggies/home

VivaVegie Society, Inc.
P.O. Box 294
Prince Street Station
New York NY 10012
Web site:
www.earthbase.org/vivivegie/

Other Web sites that become available may be found by doing a Web search.

About PETA

People for the Ethical Treatment of Animals (PETA) is an international nonprofit organization dedicated to exposing and ending animal abuse wherever it occurs through public education, litigation, research and investigations, media campaigns, lobbying, and grassroots campaigns.

PETA's many stunning victories include: the first-ever conviction of an animal experimenter for cruelty to animals; an end to car manufacturers' use of animals in crash tests; the military closing animal wound laboratories; a mainstream rejection of fur; nearly 600 cosmetics companies eliminating product-testing on animals; Taiwan passing its first-ever law against cruelty to animals; Sears Roebuck and Co. ending its sponsorship of Ringling Bros. and Barnum & Bailey Circus; a North Carolina grand jury's handing down the first-ever felony cruelty indictments against meat industry workers; and the Environmental Protection Agency changing its HPV chemical-testing program in ways that saved the lives of approximately 800,000 animals.

Operating under the credo that animals are not ours to eat, wear, experiment upon, or use for entertainment, PETA has come to the rescue of animals suffering in meat factories, slaughterhouses, animal acts, laboratories, dealer kennels, pet shops, and dissection supply houses, and on fur ranches, hunting preserves, and chains in people's backyards.

PETA depends on the support and efforts of its 650,000 members and humane people everywhere to make the world better for all animals.

If you would like information about joining PETA and/or animal rights organizations in your area, contact
    PETA
    501 Front St.
    Norfolk, VA 23510,
    or phone 757-622-PETA
You will also find much information about PETA campaigns, animal protection issues, and vegetarianism on PETA's award-winning Web site:
    www.PETA-online.org

Ask your local bookstore to carry these titles, or you may order them directly from:

Please add $3 per book for shipping.

Book Publishing Company
P.O. Box 99
Summertown, TN 38483
1-800-695-2241
www.bookpubco.com

PETA Shopping Guide for Caring Consumers - $8.95

Prisoned Chickens, Poisoned Eggs - $12.95

We're All Animals Coloring Book - $3.95

The New Farm Vegetarian Cookbook - $9.95

Cooking with PETA - $14.95

Instead of Chicken, Instead of Turkey - $12.95